BIBLE CHARACTERS AND DOCTRINES

The Corinthians to Demas
E. M. BLAIKLOCK, M.A., D.Litt.

The Church's Ministry and Ordinances
G. W. KIRBY, M.A.

William B. Eerdmans Publishing Company
Grand Rapids, Michigan

Copyright © 1975 Scripture Union
First Published 1975
First United States Edition July 1975

Printed in the United States of America

Library of Congress Cataloging in Publication Data
Main entry under title:

Bible characters and doctrines.

CONTENTS:
Cundall, A. E. God in His world. — v. 1.
Blaiklock, E. M. Adam To Esau. Crowe, P. The
God who · speaks. — Scripture and revelation.
— v. 3. Blaiklock, E. M. Nadab to Boaz. Wright,
J. S. The character of God. [etc.]
    1. Bible — Study — Text-books. I. Blaiklock, E.
M. II. Wright, John Stafford. III. Grogan,
Geoffrey.
BS605.2.B47   220'.07   72-189855
ISBN 0-8028-1471-9

SCRIPTURE UNION IN NORTH AMERICA
U.S.A.:   1716 Spruce Street
           Philadelphia, Pa. 19103
Canada: 5 Rowanwood Avenue, Toronto 5,
           Ontario

INTRODUCTION

Each volume of Bible Characters and Doctrines is divided into the right number of sections to make daily use possible, though dates are not attached to the sections because of the books' continuing use as a complete set of character studies and doctrinal expositions. The study for each day is clearly numbered and the Bible passage to be read is placed alongside it.

Sections presenting the characters and doctrines alternate throughout each book, providing balance and variety in the selected subjects. At the end of each section there is a selection of questions and themes for further study related to the material covered in the preceding readings.

Each volume will provide material for one quarter's use, with between 91 and 96 sections. Where it is suggested that two sections should be read together in order to fit the three-month period, they are marked with an asterisk.

The scheme will be completed in four years. Professor E. M. Blaiklock, who writes all the character studies, will work progressively through the Old and New Testament records. Writers of the doctrinal sections contribute to a pattern of studies drawn up by the Rev. Geoffrey Grogan, Principal of the Bible Training Institute, Glasgow, in his capacity as Co-ordinating Editor. A chart overleaf indicates how the doctrinal sections are planned.

In this series biblical quotations are normally taken from the RSV unless otherwise identified. Occasionally Professor Blaiklock provides his own translation of the biblical text.

DOCTRINAL STUDY SCHEME

	Year 1	Year 2	Year 3	Year 4
First Quarter	The God who Speaks	Man and Sin	The Work of Christ	The Kingdom and the Church
Second Quarter	God in His World	Law and Grace	Righteousness in Christ	The Mission of the Church
Third Quarter	The Character of God	The Life of Christ	Life in Christ	The Church's Ministry and Ordinances
Fourth Quarter	The Holy Trinity	The Person of Christ	The Holy Spirit	The Last Things

DOCTRINAL STUDIES
THE CHURCH'S MINISTRY AND ORDINANCES

6

CHARACTER STUDIES
THE CORINTHIANS TO DEMAS

THE CHURCH'S MINISTRY AND ORDINANCES

Introduction

It is unfortunate that 'minister' has come to have a special technical sense for the Church today, so that a distinction is made between 'the ministry' and the laity. Such a distinction is foreign to the New Testament, which makes it clear that the Church is the Body of Christ and that there is a ministry for every member of that Body. The great spiritual principles of Christian service are illustrated time and again in the New Testament, especially in the ministry of the apostle Paul, but their highest illustration is to be found in Christ Himself. We should remember, too, that the New Testament doctrine of the ministry has its roots in the Old Testament.

Excessive emphasis on ritual in the Church has often proved destructive of real spirituality, indeed it may even be a symptom of a spiritual malaise. God has however given His Church two simple ordinances or sacraments—some Christians prefer the one word and some the other—which illustrate the gospel. Like the Word of God, they are means of grace. It is important that we understand them biblically.

THE CHURCH'S MINISTRY AND ORDINANCES

Divine and Human Shepherds in the Old Testament

Introduction

In Old Testament times the shepherd was a familiar figure in Palestine. It is not surprising therefore that God is frequently described as the Shepherd of Israel. Good shepherds were renowned for the care and love which they showed towards their flock; protecting them from danger and providing for their sustenance. The term shepherd came to be used of those who were called upon to care for the people of God. Thus Moses was so described (Isa. 63.11). There were those who failed to act as true shepherds to the people, and these are consistently denounced. The faithless shepherd stands under the judgement of God (Jer. 23.1–4; 25.32–38; Ezek. 34).

The same metaphor is carried on to the New Testament where Christ Himself is pictured as the Good Shepherd (John 10).

1: The Shepherd Psalm

Psalm 23

The eastern shepherd occupied a unique position in relation to his flock. Early in the morning he would lead them from their fold to pasture-lands. Throughout the day he would guard them against attacks from wild animals or robbers. At night-fall he would lead them back to the security of the fold. Should one of the lambs be unable to keep pace with the rest of the flock he would pick it up and carry it on his shoulders. Should one of the flock go astray he would search for it until he found it. The sheep and the shepherd were intimately related. The sheep knew their shepherd, and would answer to their names.

In this most familiar of all psalms, David is saying that God is his Shepherd. In saying this he is implying that men need shepherding; that we are, in fact, like sheep all too prone to go astray (Isa. 53.6). The psalmist goes on to say that since the Lord is his Shepherd he will not be in want—his needs will be met.

Even in times of danger he will be cared for and protected. An experienced shepherd might take his flock from one pasture to another along a narrow path with perhaps a sheer drop on one side and rugged rocks on the other. So men in life may be constantly surrounded with difficulties and dangers, but with divine companionship they need have no fear.

The eastern shepherd carried a *shebet*, which was club-like in shape, having a large knob on one end. He also carried a staff. With the *shebet* he could defend his sheep against wild beasts, and he might sometimes use his staff to rescue them when they had become entangled in undergrowth, and at other times to give them a gentle tap to ensure that they kept in step with the rest.

This is a person-to-person psalm. It has been said that the heart of religion lies in its personal pronouns. Here are pictured the three great blessings of provision, direction and communion. What more can we need or desire with such a Shepherd as this, a Shepherd who is at one and the same time guide, physician and protector?

Christians can re-echo the psalmist's words with greater emphasis since the Lord Jesus Christ declared Himself to be the 'Good Shepherd' and was prepared to suffer the awful death of the Cross in order to bring us back to God. He has a shepherd's heart of compassion, a shepherd's eye that watches ceaselessly over His flock, and a shepherd's faithfulness that never forsakes or forgets His own. Furthermore, He has a shepherd's strength to lift up those who have fallen.

2: Israel's Plea to her Shepherd

Psalm 80

Opinions vary as to the date of the composition of this psalm. One widely held view is that it was written by a poet from Judah after the deportation of the northern tribes to Assyria, either before or during the Babylonian exile. The 'boar' in v. 13 is probably Assyria. The recurring refrain (3, 7, 19) divides the psalm into three parts.

The first part (1–3) is a prayer addressed to the Shepherd of Israel, seeking the restoration of the divine favour. Jacob had seen God in this role and when speaking to his sons prior to his death he referred to 'the Shepherd, the Rock of Israel' (Gen. 49.24).

In the next section (4–7) the psalmist appears to be in a somewhat querulous mood deploring the fact that Israel has become a laughing-stock to her neighbours (6).

In the remaining part of the psalm (8–19) Israel is seen as the chosen vine, which has now become desolate, and the psalmist looks ahead to happier days when that vine will again flourish.

The whole psalm is full of pleas on Israel's behalf, with a wistful looking back to days of prosperity and blessing. The psalmist pleads that the Shepherd will give heed to the bleatings of the sheep and come to their aid.

There is a certain lack of penitence in this psalm. Israel is sorry for herself, but there is little indication that she feels entirely to blame for her sad condition. In days of spiritual and moral declension many of the pleas found in this psalm will find an echo in our hearts, and particularly the recurring refrain.

It is significant that the psalmist makes his appeal to God on the basis of His unique relationship to Israel. This finds an echo in the words of the hymn writer,

> *His love in time past forbids me to think*
> *He will leave me at last in trouble to sink.*

Dr. Graham Scroggie aptly entitles this psalm 'Prayer for the recovery of a lost past'. One is reminded of the reference in the prophecy of Joel to 'the years which the swarming locust has eaten' (Joel 2.25).

The reference to 'the man of thy right hand' (17) may well have had a contemporary application, but it finds its fullest expression in the person of Jesus Christ (cf. Heb. 1.13). At meals the master of the feast would place the most honoured guest on his right hand.

If, as has been said, Psa. 80 gives us 'a permanent picture of Israel's woeful condition when banished from God's presence and scattered among the nations', it should also serve as a warning and a rebuke to backsliding Christians whose only plea must likewise be: 'Restore us, O God'.

3: The Lord as the Good Shepherd

Ezekiel 34

It is quite customary in the Old Testament to find rulers described as shepherds, (cf. Isa. 44.28; Jer. 2.8; 10.21; 23.1–6; 25.34–38; Mic. 5.4, 5; Zech. 11.4–17). The very word 'shepherd' suggests both leadership, and caring. Ezekiel has some strong words to say about those shepherds, who, instead of caring for the people

13

had, in fact, exploited them. Such shepherds would receive the divine judgement. They had shown none of the pastoral qualities which were required of them, and instead of keeping the flock together they had allowed them to become scattered. The result was that the people were, in effect, like sheep without a shepherd. Nevertheless, God does still care for His sheep, even though the shepherds appointed by Him have failed. In this passage God is represented as taking on the role of Shepherd to His people. He will seek out the particularly needy sheep—those who have wandered away, and those who are ailing. God is seen here as a God of infinite compassion, tender and loving.

The picture in the latter part of the chapter is of the good shepherd, who will distinguish between the good and bad sheep in His flock. Verses 23 and 24 point to the Messianic Shepherd who gathers the scattered flock together, and leads them into peace and prosperity. This Shepherd was symbolized in earlier times in the person of King David, but he is not merely the historical David resurrected. Christians see in this picture Christ, in His future role as Messianic ruler, ushering in the golden age.

The latter part of the chapter pictures this golden age of unprecedented blessing. It may be compared with similar passages elsewhere (cf. Isa. **11**.6–9; Hos. **2**.22; Joel **3**.18; Amos **9**.13ff.; Zech. **8**.12). The new era is essentially different, because of a change of shepherd—the blessings envisaged are essentially linked with the coming of the Messiah. Christians usually interpret these blessings spiritually, seeing in them representations of God's gifts to us in Christ. The 'new age' is marked by a 'covenant of peace' (25). This is to be understood in a positive sense pointing to good relationships. God's people will enjoy security under the divine protection. Fears are dispelled. Blessings will abound. The glorious climax to it all is to be seen in the recognition that the covenant between God and the people is once more established (30).

This 'new covenant' is completely unconditional, since it rests solely upon the faithfulness of God. Its provisions are outlined by several of the Old Testament prophets, including Ezekiel (cf. especially Jer. **31**.31–34). Within the New Covenant were promises of both earthly and spiritual blessings. In his commentary on the Epistle to the Hebrews, Professor F. F. Bruce remarks: 'The first covenant provided a measure of atonement and remission for sins committed under it, but it was incapable of providing "eternal redemption"; this was a blessing which had to await the inaugu-

14

ration of the New Covenant which embodies God's promise to His people, "I will forgive their iniquity and their sin will I remember no more" (Jer. **31**.34). The covenant is an everlasting one. Even though its spiritual blessings are already being enjoyed by believers, its complete fulfilment is yet to come.

4: The Rejected Shepherd
Zechariah 11.4–17; 13.7–9

In these passages the spiritual leaders of the people are once more spoken of as shepherds. In ch. **11** Israel and Judah are condemned for their rejection of the Good Shepherd. The message which begins with v. 4 is addressed to Zechariah who is in the line of true shepherds in contrast with the false. The flock of which the prophet is commanded to take charge had been handed over to the slaughterer without a moment's hesitation. Those who had sold the sheep in this way had congratulated themselves on the good prices they had received for them. While Israel is 'the flock doomed to slaughter', even so there is to be found within the nation a faithful remnant ('Grace' v. 7; cf. Rom. **11**.5). From the outset, however, it is clear that the shepherd's effort to save the flock will be a failure.

In the vision Zechariah takes two staves, Grace (lit. Beauty) and Union (lit. Bands). The first staff spoke of the relationship of the flock to their divine Shepherd, while the second symbolized the union of Israel and Judah (cf. Ezek. **37**.15–23). The three shepherds (8) may well be three kings, and the mention of 'one month' probably signifies a short space of time. The people are to be left to the fate they have brought upon themselves. God's favour and gracious protection can no longer be assumed. The people as a whole had failed to appreciate the best of shepherds.

Having ceased to serve as a good shepherd the prophet now assumes the role of a worthless shepherd (15), and foresees a reign of terror in the land. As has been pointed out 'if Yahweh is not received as a Shepherd, then another will be, and that other will be a shepherd of doom.'

The immediate fulfilment of vs. 4–14 may have been the period of anarchy which followed on the murder of Pekah, while in vs. 15–17 we may have a reference to the reign of the 'worthless shepherd' Hoshea.

The mention of thirty pieces of silver (12)—the price of an injured slave—reminds us of the price paid at the betrayal of

Jesus. He too was rejected by the very people whom He had come to shepherd. One lesson emerges clearly from this otherwise rather difficult passage—Christ cannot be rejected with impunity. As Thomas V. Moore in his commentary on Zechariah observes: 'God may bear long with the wicked, but there is a point where the piling avalanche will cease to be held back, and descend in fearful ruin.'

Some commentators have suggested the two verses (7–9) in ch. 13 might appropriately come at the end of ch. 11. We have here a description of the divine chastisement which is to come upon the people. Whatever the immediate significance of these words may have been, their complete fulfilment is found in Christ. When the Good Shepherd was smitten even His own sheep were scandalized and fled (Matt. 26.31; Mark 14.27; John 16.32). Verse 8 was tragically fulfilled in the destruction of Jerusalem by the Roman army in A.D. 70. We learn from v. 9 that the smaller portion of the people who are saved, are nevertheless called upon to pass through great trials.

Questions and themes for study and discussion on Studies 1–4

1. How did David benefit from being under the Shepherd's tender care?
2. What was the state of the nation when she had strayed from the Shepherd of Israel?
3. Contrast the ways of the shepherds of Israel with the Lord's care for His flock.

CHARACTER STUDIES

5: The Corinthians

Acts 18.1–11; 1 Corinthians 1.1–16

Paul's foundation of the church at Corinth was one of the signal triumphs of his career. 'The church of God which is at Corinth', is a striking phrase, for Corinth was the most notoriously vicious of the cities of the ancient world. And yet the grace of God found lodging there (4), and with divine incongruity there were those found in the evil cosmopolitan port on the isthmus who were called 'saints', and 'sanctified in Christ Jesus' (2).

Along with Rome, Corinth was more like a cosmopolitan modern city than any other of the score or more of towns and cities which find mention in the New Testament. We also know more about its church, its people and its problems, than we know of any other church in the New Testament. In a world which is becoming increasingly urbanized, Corinth is a significant and vital study.

The society in which it operates colours a church for good and ill. The strength and weakness of a city find reflection in the problems, the qualities, and the defects of the church which is drawn from its multitude, and Corinth clearly illustrates this fact. That pseudo-intellectual, sex-ridden, argumentative, yet enterprising society, produced a church prone to faction, division, controversy, and which sometimes is quite horrifying. The early Church is sometimes idealized. Corinth is evidence enough that most of the problems which afflict the twentieth-century congregation were known in Corinth, from denominationalism to scepticism over the physical resurrection of Christ.

The lessons are many. God can redeem in the most corrupt environment; God can redeem the worst sinners; God redeems progressively. Paul saw the potentialities. He looked to the end. He never lost hope. That is why he begins his letter with words of gracious confidence. He sets forth the remedy as he writes. Christ is mentioned eight times in these eight verses. He is preparing the way for the great evangelical statements which close the chapter and come to a climax in the testimony of 2.2. An exalted Christ, uplifted and undiminished, is the one solution to the problems of the Church.

Paul turns rapidly to the first major problem of Corinth, that

17

of division. The city was a melting-pot, a tangle and mixture of races. The languages of all the Mediterranean were heard in the streets. The church, which, like the net (Matt. 13.47), drew all manner of fish ashore, had gathered its congregation from people of different races, of different social background, of different orders of society. There were Jews and Greeks, Italian traders, Phoenician sailors, girls emancipated from the temple-service of Aphrodite . . . It was natural enough that tastes would differ and variant loyalties emerge. Perhaps there is no church in the New Testament whose members, as men and women, emerge more clearly from the words of the great man who sought in wisdom to meet their needs.

6: The Corinthians Again

1 Corinthians 1.17–25; 2.1–10

Three groups of Corinthians emerge from this passage, representing three attitudes towards Paul's preaching, and perhaps continuing to reflect attitudes within the church. Verse 18 might be rendered: 'The message of the cross is, to those who are destroying themselves, foolishness, but to those who are being saved it is the power of God.' The present tenses should be stressed. 'In the language of the New Testament,' says Lightfoot, 'salvation is a thing of the past, a thing of the present, and a thing of the future . . . The divorce of morality and religion is fostered by failing to note this, and so laying the whole stress on either the past or the future—on the first call or on the final change.'

Such was its simplicity. Christianity is a faith, and faith implies the staking of the life on a conviction, a conviction that God revealed Himself in Christ. The Corinthians, prone to philosophic speculation, baulked at such simplicity. Most modern error had its ancient counterpart, and that was always so. Paul quotes Isa. 29.14 in illustration.

The Jews wanted 'a sign'. It was an endemic malady. Theudas, in A.D. 45, led multitudes into the wilderness and disaster with the promise that he would divide the Jordan like another Joshua or Elisha (Acts 5.36). Almost twenty years later, a certain 'Egyptian' led 30,000 dupes out on to the Mount of Olives with the promise that he would destroy the walls of Jerusalem (Acts 21.38). Their misconception of the Messiah gave rise to this quirk. A humble Christ, who offered no vast demonstrations, and who called for self-abandonment, 'stumbled' them.

The Greeks sought philosophy and found the cult of the crucified absurd. The 'wondrous cross' is a phrase which baffles their successors. The Greeks could not see how the love of God, and the depth of human sin, could not be shown in a less shattering way than both were shown on Calvary. Pride and intellectual arrogance is the crippling fault of the 'Greeks'. And yet the Greeks for whom Paul wrote had no substitute. 'How can I say more unless I have the word of some God?' the great Socrates had asked four and a half centuries before, after he had spent his last day piling reason on reason for believing in immortality. The Word came, was made flesh (John 1.14), died and rose again. This was the gospel (2.2) which Paul preached. There is no other Christ, no Christianity without a cross. The Corinthians stood challenged and confronted.

When Paul came to Corinth he was determined not to pander to the Corinthian love of words. The itinerant teachers, who earned a living by rhetorical display and dexterity of speech, had a happy hunting ground in the city of the isthmus. Having been taken for such a person in Athens, Paul was now resolved to abandon the arts of persuasion so carefully taught by the Greeks, skilled though he was in such oratory (e.g. Acts 17.22–29; 24.10–21). Nor would he rephrase his message in the terms of an ephemeral philosophy. Christ, Paul knew, would remain. The sophists would pass. 'Their poor displays of wisdom,' said Cicero of them, 'only prick like pins ... they do not change the heart, and the listeners go away just as they came.'

7: The Leaders

1 Corinthians 3

Corinthian controversy did not involve the leaders round whose names the unwelcome loyalties grew. Peter has a charming word to say of Paul (2 Pet. 3.15f.). There is no sign of division between Paul and Apollos. Christian workers are partners in God's enterprise. The reaper cannot claim the crop, as the Lord told His men at the well of Sychar (John 4.36–38). Paul recognized that his eighteen months in Corinth had been but a scattering of the good seed. He is tacitly referring to a Galilean parable of Christ. Apollos had stayed on to foster and bring to maturity the seed which had found fertile ground. Christ would reap the crop.

This surely is ideal evangelism. It is a blessed partnership of faithful proclamation, devoted pastoral care, and God's Spirit active in the church.

There is a touch of Paul's experience in the pictures of the strong foundation and the temple. Paul had come to Corinth from Athens. He wrote from Ephesus. In Athens, Corinth, and Ephesus, great temples rested on vast blocks of hewn stone. The Greeks knew well that it was what lay beneath which gave steadiness, permanence, and grace to what stood above. The beauty of the Parthenon, Athena's great Doric shrine, still astonishes the world. Its foundations, firm and unshaken after twenty-four centuries, rest on the great rock of the Acropolis. The picture of it was surely in Paul's mind, as also a saying of Christ, (Matt. 16.18) when he wrote to Corinth of 'no other foundation'.

Above the ruined market-place of Corinth, there still stands on a low ridge with a far view down the Corinthian Gulf, a few columns of Apollo's temple. The Romans left the building standing, alone amid the desolation, when they sacked Corinth in 146 B.C. A century later, when Julius Caesar rebuilt the city, the ancient Doric shrine still stood, dominating the city centre, as its remnants do today. 'You,' Paul tells the church, 'are God's temple in the place.' The Greek temple was kept scrupulously clean. The Greek temple was simple, and housed only one deity. It stood high for all to see, Athena at Athens, Poseidon on the high promontory of Sounion, Apollo above Corinth's agora . . . No Corinthian would miss the point. Let them build on the one foundation. There was no other. Let them build grandly and conspicuously, a clean dwelling-place for God, unshared, elegant, enduring.

It is fine strong writing, with words and imagery relevant to the experience of the one who wrote, and of those who read. A man writes well when he writes from conviction, and with a burning passion to persuade. And such a man, deeply versed in the interwoven cultures of his day, caught in a great historic movement, and fervent for a cause, frequently writes prose of purpose and power beyond the need and call of its immediate occasion.

8: Paul's Courtesy

1 Corinthians 4

Paul has dealt kindly with the philosophical pretensions of some in the Corinthian church. Any close student of Plato and the Stoics can recognize in Paul's first four chapters allusions, and easy half-references to the writings of both, which make it clear enough that he knew far more of philosophic thought than the small group in the isthmus church which despised the simple presentation of the message.

And yet observe in this chapter how gently and humbly he deals with them. Paul was, as we have again and again had occasion to note, superbly educated. He was willing, none the less, to be called a fool for Christ's sake—in such contrast to those in the small church who imagined they had outgrown his teaching. Verses 11 to 13 form a moving picture of what it meant to be a Christian—indeed, what it still means for some. There is a persecution which seeks to inflict pain on the body. There is a more cruel and subtle persecution which seeks to hurt the mind—the high contempt of the academic for one committed to a faith, the covert sneer against the man who holds fast to his uprightness in a bent and crooked world . . . Paul knew it all.

There is no hot scorn for those who added pain to what the world at large had already inflicted. There is no sharper tooth than that of ingratitude, but Paul merely seeks, forgetting his deep hurt, to turn them to self-examination and to thankfulness. They had been blessed by many who had sought to teach them—Peter himself, and the brilliant Apollos among the rest. Paul was their father in Christ, and there could only be one.

Hence the sending of the well-loved Timothy, instructed to tell them again of those simplicities of Christ which were all they needed to know. There is some evidence, if references in the second letter are read aright, that Timothy came, but was not well-received. C. G. Findlay remarks that Timothy was Paul's complement, as Melancthon was of Luther. Such a reception for his beloved ambassador would grieve Paul deeply, and some wonder is due that one so strong in his views and his loyalties, no less than in the firm insistence on the absolute integrity of his gospel, should deal with a disordered and falsely proud congregation with courtesy, restraint, and reserve so notable.

Paul was a personality of manifold facets. Such characters are too commonly and too shallowly judged on the evidence of one controverted opinion, or one incident such as the clash with Barnabas. Paul had schooled his vehemence to gentleness, his immense intelligence to patience with the foolish, and his swift decisiveness to humility.

9: The Weaker Brothers

1 Corinthians 8

The theme of v.7 continues to its climax in the fine closing words of the chapter. The dangerous minority in Corinth which claimed 'knowledge', and turned Christian liberty into an excuse for licence, lacked love and care for others. The intellectual is commonly impatient with the emotional, and both types were present in Corinth. In the former the head outran the heart. The latter reversed the process. It takes both to make a church. It is also true that in the balanced personality both head and heart, the intellect and the emotions, have their place, part and partnership.

Love is the answer, and the reader catches the first notes of the theme which is to reach its climax in ch. **13**. Pride is the vice which dogs the intellectual, and there was pride, as well as lack of feeling, in the Christian who confidently and contemptuously 'sat at meat in the idol's temple', taking part in a pagan ceremony because it was meaningless. Another, following his example, as the emotionally bent are prone to do, is damaged in the act, trapped into a weakening compromise with conscience, and marred in his Christian integrity.

Paul's comment is still valid. In modern society the problem may have shifted its ground, but day by day brings situations which are similar in import and solution. Hughes, author of *Tom Brown's Schooldays*, wrote of his hero, Arnold of Rugby: 'He taught us that in this wonderful world no one can tell which of his actions is indifferent and which is not. He taught us that, by a thoughtless word or look we may lead astray a brother for whom Christ died.' This is Paul's meaning. 'All things are lawful', but through all and over all such liberty stands the constraining power of Christian love.

Why, it might be asked in conclusion, did not Paul quote the Jerusalem Decree which had ruled in the matter of 'idol meat'? (Acts **15**.29). It is probable that the Judaizing party had so disregarded it that Paul himself treated it as a dead letter. Or else he regarded the decree as inoperable in Europe and in a fully Greek community.

But observe again the tender care for 'the weaker'. We are learning to know Paul. Learn by heart the last verse. It has much to say.

10: Paul's Testimony

1 Corinthians 9

Paul has made it clear that he cared enough for others to be willing not to claim a freedom if that claim could cause misunderstanding or lead some other person into difficulty or wrongdoing. He proceeds to illustrate his attitude by some remarks which are a light upon his character and manner of life. The theme becomes vividly autobiographical.

He claims that, as a witness of the resurrected Christ, he was an apostle, and therefore entitled to such privileges as befell an apostle—to be a charge, for example, on the churches for maintenance. To avoid all jealousy, to by-pass all criticism by lesser folk in the Christian community, he had foregone such privileges, and earned his own living in humble employment. The Judaistic party in the church were, no doubt, denying Paul's genuine apostleship. But note the tact with which Paul, having vindicated firmly his own rights, does not make his deliberate waiving of them an embarrassment to his fellow-workers.

He acted thus because he had a consuming passion—to win men for Christ. He has renounced much in order that, untrammelled by obligations, he might meet all classes on conditions of equality. Hence the oft-quoted (and not infrequently misapplied) words of vs. 19–22. The words mean that he sought to approach the various classes and conditions of people he met with understanding of their outlook, sympathy for their difficulties, mercy for their prejudices, patience with their preoccupations. He 'spoke their language' in more senses than one. He sought to share their interests, discover points of contact, make them sense his concern. Perhaps it was an over-emphasis in this delicate task which led him into the error we have noted, and be too ready to conform to a Jewish preoccupation—with the consequent misadventure in Jerusalem. But it is a noble ideal, and we have seen it illustrated again and again.

It required the discipline of the athlete, a matter with which Paul closes the chapter. He often refers to the Greek games with the demands for asceticism, training, perseverance, and dedicated energy for which they necessarily called. God's athlete could do no less than those who strove for the crown of wild olive.

Questions and themes for study and discussion on Studies 5–10

1. A church and its environment.

2. Salvation as past, present and future.
3. Philosophy cannot produce a theology but sound theology can produce a philosophy.
4. 'The grace of God is in courtesy'—Belloc.
5. The weaker brother today—for example, in relation to alcohol.
6. 'All things to all men'—how does this principle apply today?

THE CHURCH'S MINISTRY AND ORDINANCES

Christ the Pattern of all Ministry

Introduction

A key verse in the New Testament is Mark 10.45 in which our Lord makes clear that He had come 'not to be served, but to serve'. Elsewhere He pointed out that He was among His disciples 'as one who serves' (Luke 22.27). Just before His crucifixion He washed His disciples' feet. In the classic passage of the letter to the Philippians the apostle points out that He took 'the form of a servant'. It is clear that all who profess to follow Him and to serve under Him must of necessity see themselves as servants, since He Himself has set a pattern for all Christian ministry.

11: The Temptation of Jesus

Luke 4.1–21

In this chapter we have a condensed record of the first year of our Lord's ministry. We do not know precisely the amount of time covered by these incidents, but we are given a glimpse of the sort of work He did in the months immediately following His baptism and temptation.

The temptation, while not a part of His public ministry was, nevertheless, part of God's preparation for it. As so often in our experience as Christians, our Lord found that a time of great spiritual blessing may be followed by one of great testing.

There can be no doubt as to the reality of Christ's temptations, even though the manner in which they presented themselves must remain a mystery. Christ found Satan to be very real and in His battle with him He wielded the Sword of the Spirit, which is the Word of God (Eph. 6.17). He referred to God's will as being the all-important consideration, and steadfastly resisted the temptation to depart from, or short-circuit it.

The Devil tempted Him to satisfy His natural appetite by turning stones into bread, but had He yielded to this temptation, there would have been no Gethsemane and no Calvary. Christ was not concerned primarily with His physical needs, but, rather,

25

to fulfil the spiritual purpose for which He had come into the world. The Devil offered Jesus the kingdoms of this world if only He would bow down and worship him, but, here again, the Lord resisted this short-cut to the achievement of the Messianic purpose.

In the third temptation as recorded by Luke, Satan urged Christ to throw Himself down from the pinnacle of the temple. This time the devil himself quoted Scripture, suggesting that He could count on supernatural protection if He would only follow this course. Christ knew that this was no way to draw men to Himself, and, once more, He steadfastly resisted the idea of by-passing God's plan.

The events recorded in vs. 14–22 are only found in Luke's Gospel. They relate to the first visit Jesus paid, after entering on His public ministry, to the synagogue in Nazareth, where He had been brought up. It is noteworthy that His regular custom was to worship in the synagogue every sabbath day. There was special significance in the passage of scripture which He read on this occasion. In voicing the words of Isa. 61 He sought to impress on His Jewish hearers the true character of their Messiah. This prophecy would not find fulfilment in an earthly ruler wielding purely temporal power. He announced that the prophetic passage which He had just read was that day being fulfilled in the presence of His hearers.

No doubt in the synagogue were many of His relatives and friends and it seems that a deep impression was made upon them by the way He spoke. Nevertheless, we do know from other parts of scripture that our Lord was subsequently rejected by His fellow citizens—no prophet is accepted in his own country. Christ's experience in this connection has all too often been repeated in the experience of His disciples.

12: Dealing with Critics

Matthew 12.9–21; 2 Timothy 2.23–26

Much of the opposition which Jesus encountered from religious leaders took the form of 'loaded' questions designed to catch Him out. Often in dealing with these questions He Himself would pose another, the effect of which would show up the absurdity of the original question. One of the points on which the Jewish leaders concentrated was our Lord's attitude to the sabbath.

They appeared to be scandalized when on one occasion He and His disciples went through the cornfields on the sabbath day, and plucked ears of grain because they were hungry. Often those who are bent on opposing the work of God persist in their opposition even though their questions are dealt with. Although Christ clearly answered Jewish criticisms regarding His conduct on the sabbath day, nevertheless, 'the Pharisees went out and took counsel against him, how to destroy him' (Matt. 12.14).

The apostle Paul repeatedly warned Timothy against allowing himself to become involved in 'senseless controversy'. He points out that arguing for arguing's sake serves no useful purpose, but stirs up needless strife. Striving for its own sake has no place in the life of a servant of God (cf. Matt. 12.19). Our aim should always be to win over our opponents rather than antagonize them, and in any Christian leader meekness and patient forbearance should be apparent. In cases where people have been led into error the Christian is concerned to correct them with 'gentleness' in the hope that God may bring them to repentance (2 Tim. 2.25). The Devil has been described as both an intoxicator and captivator of men's minds. He delights to assume the role of an 'angel of light', and in so doing he makes false teaching attractive in the eyes of men. In the final analysis, only God Himself can take the scales from the eyes of those blinded by the Devil in this way, so that they come to see the truth.

The right way to handle opponents should be a matter of concern to all Christian leaders. Paul in giving advice to Timothy foresees that by being kindly disposed rather than aggressive one is more likely to win them over and not antagonize them. It should be the aim of the Christian to be the means, under God, of bringing people to repentance and deliverance from Satan's power.

A Christian worker needs to be able to differentiate between the genuine seeker after truth and the person who loves asking questions and is not over-interested in the answers. Furthermore, he needs to avoid the time-consuming luxury of getting embroiled in controversies which are likely to produce no conclusive solutions.

13: The Servant Role
Mark 10.35–45; Luke 22.24–30

It is significant that when we speak of the work of our Lord here on earth we usually describe it as His earthly 'ministry'. Service was the hallmark of all that He did. He declared 'The Son of Man came not to be served, but to serve, and to give His life as a ransom for many' (Mark 10.45). The word translated 'to serve', the Greek *diakoneo*, literally means 'to wait on tables, to function as a servant'. He told His disciples quite clearly that He was among them as one who served. When in the Upper Room, on the night before His crucifixion, He stooped to wash His disciples' feet, He said to them, 'If I then, your Lord and Teacher, have washed your feet, you also ought to wash one another's feet. For I have given you an example, that you also should do as I have done to you'. (John 13.14f.). He pointed out that while worldly rulers were preoccupied with their status and their authority, this was not to be the case with His followers (Mark 10.42–44). Ministry to Him was literally service.

In the light both of our Lord's example and of His teaching it is somewhat ironical that today the accent is often placed on ministerial status, whereas the pattern of Christian ministry which He so clearly set was one of lowly service. He Himself was happy to take upon Himself 'the form of a servant'. He saw ministry not in terms of status but of function. No doubt He often had in His mind the Servant Songs of Isaiah (42.1–4; 49.1–6; 50.4–7; 52.13–53.12). In them He saw a foreshadowing of His own ministry which was to call for lowly obedience and vicarious suffering. The concept of the servant was never far from His mind, and all the more so towards the end of His earthly life. Because the Lord Jesus Himself was a servant, His disciples should walk in His steps (Matt. 10.24f.). As J. K. S. Reid has pointed out, 'The prototype for the ministry is our Lord Himself; the pattern for all the New Testament has to say about the ministry is what our Lord has to say about His ministry.'

It is significant that in the Christian Church two of the words used to describe those occupying positions of leadership mean servant. Thus, we describe the pastor of a local church as a 'minister' and those who assist him are sometimes given the title 'deacons'. 'Minister' comes from a Latin word meaning servant, and deacon from a Greek word meaning the same.

It is particularly sad when Christian leaders contend for position, as did James and John. As someone has said: 'The greatest prelate in the church is he who is most conformable to the example of Christ, by humility, charity and continual attendance on his flock and who looks on himself as a servant to the children of God' (Quesnel).

14: The Good Shepherd

John 10.1–30

Our Lord had been accusing the Pharisees of spiritual blindness, and He followed up His indictment by relating the parable of the sheepfold and the Good Shepherd. Since the Pharisees had proved to be blind leaders they could also be described as bogus shepherds.

Throughout Scripture the flock is always regarded as ultimately belonging to God, though He may entrust the care of it to others. Down the centuries there have been good and bad shepherds. The sign of a bad shepherd was that he did not care for his sheep, and for that reason was under the divine judgement (Jer. 23.1f.; Ezek. 34.1–6).

Religious leaders have often failed their followers. In every generation we have to be careful to avoid 'the spirit of the hireling' who lacks a sense of responsibility, is cowardly in face of danger, and shows no real concern for his flock. In contrast, the good shepherd knows his sheep, sends them out, shows personal concern for them, and is even prepared to die for them. The sheep, for their part, know him and recognize his voice, and are ready to follow him.

Verse 16 has been the subject of considerable discussion. Two different Greek words are used and in the RSV this fact is rightly recognized by the use of two different English words 'fold' and 'flock'. The sheep 'not of this fold' are presumably non-Jewish believers. Some early Jewish Christians made the mistake of thinking that all believers should be incorporated into the Jewish Christian community and be compelled to submit to Jewish rites and customs (Acts 15). We learn from this verse that the flock of God will be made up of many different groups and certainly not confined to Jewish believers. The Church is truly a multi-racial society.

15: The Lord's Prayer

John 17

We often describe the prayer Christ taught His disciples as 'the Lord's prayer'. In fact, He Himself never prayed it since it was not applicable to Him. He had no sins to confess and, therefore, no need to ask for forgiveness.

The prayer in this chapter could be more accurately described as 'the Lord's prayer', since we know that He Himself prayed it and only He could have done so. In the first five verses Christ is praying for Himself, whilst the remainder of the prayer is for His disciples. The prayer was uttered in the presence of His disciples in the 'upper room' shortly before His crucifixion. There was no sense of failure or defeat on His part as He contemplated His impending death, but rather the note of triumph. He was about to bring to a successful conclusion the work the Father had given Him. Soon He would be leaving this earth, and the responsibility for proclaiming the good news which He was making possible through His death and subsequent resurrection must rest with His followers. This, then, is Christ's prayer for His Church.

It is significant that His first petition is for the Church's holiness. While His disciples must remain in the world they must nevertheless not be contaminated by it. They represent a community distinct from the world. Jesus prayed that God would preserve their essential holiness (15). Christians are called to be 'holy' people in an 'unholy' world (Phil. 2.15).

Christ now turns to the Church's mission, the very reason for its continued existence in the world (18). The Church plays an essential part in God's plan for the salvation of the world. The Church in every generation needs to be reminded of its missionary vocation.

Next our Lord turns to the Church's unity. He longs for the absolute unity of His people. The inherent unity of Father and Son in the Godhead is to be the pattern for the essential unity of believers (22). It must be stressed that this prayer clearly envisages those who are genuine believers (20). It is a unity in the truth. There is a tendency today to look for organizational unity without adequate attention being paid to the biblical basis which true unity demands. Only the Spirit of God can create unity, but Christians have a responsibility to maintain it (Eph. 4.3). Christ's love for us is to be the standard by which we gauge our love for one another.

16: The Strong and the Weak

Romans 15.1–13

Here the apostle is pointing out the responsibilities we as Christians have for one another. There must be mutual concern. Christ is the supreme example of one who did not 'please' or put Himself first (3). Throughout the New Testament there is stress upon living in harmony with one another, and so glorifying God. Note that the word 'please' occurs three times in the opening verses of this chapter. As Bishop Moule has pointed out, this word does not suggest a servile and compromising deference to human opinion, but 'the unselfish and watchful aim to meet half way, if possible, the thought and feeling of a fellow disciple'.

During our Lord's earthly ministry His work was mainly restricted to Jewish people, and in that sense, He was 'a servant to the circumcised' (8). Nevertheless, His purpose was that Jews and Gentiles should unite in praising God, and that Gentiles should join with Jews in acknowledging Him (8–12). In v. 13 Paul uses the title, 'God of hope', and speaks of peace and joy as blessings which belong to the Kingdom of God. Even though Christians may have the clearest intellectual grasp of the gospel it is only through the Holy Spirit that they are enabled to enjoy, in this life, the blessings of the life to come. In this verse we have a picture of the ideal Christian life—being in touch with God, filled with joy and peace and overflowing with hope—a life lived in the power of the Holy Spirit. In so far as Christians keep before them such an ideal they will discover the secret of true spiritual unity and the superficial differences between them will pale into insignificance.

Paul here sets out his 'philosophy' of Christian service. There are many different words and phrases which relate to effective co-operation in Christian work. There were issues then, as there are today, which tend to divide the Lord's people. The apostle makes the point that all who truly believe in Christ, whether Jews or Gentiles, are to receive one another in the Lord regardless of their backgrounds. He calls for mutual tolerance and under-standing. Harmony should be the keynote of relationships be-tween Christians, whether strong or weak, Jewish or Gentile. Heathen observers said of the early Christians: 'Behold how these Christians love one another.' When believers are God-centred in their thinking, and truly desirous to do His will and reveal His glory, they will be patient with one another (5f.). We are not, of course, to tolerate evil or blatant error, but we must be ready at times to 'agree to differ' with other Christians on matters of secondary importance, which are open to question— 'In things essential unity, in things doubtful liberty, in all things charity.' How sad it must make the Lord when His children fight over matters on which differing opinions may legitimately be held! Real peace is impossible when we are at cross-purposes with fellow Christians.

17: The Divine Condescension

Philippians 2.1–11

This portion contains one of the outstanding Christological passages in the New Testament. It has been suggested that we have here an ancient hymn in rhythmical form (5–11). The context is an appeal for spiritual unity and the demonstration of humility. It is helpful to read the opening verses in a modern rendering. In ancient Greece lowliness of mind was an attitude worthy only of slaves, yet it is an essentially Christian virtue. Those who truly have the mind of Christ are delivered from self-seeking and self-centredness.

The apostle traces the steps which Christ took from the Father's throne to the Cross of shame—seven rugged steps. First, He was in the form of God, or, as we might say, essentially God. He possessed the very essence of Deity from all eternity (cf. John 1.1f.; 8.58; 17.5). Next, He regarded equality with God as something which rightly belonged to Him, and for which He had no need to strive. It is not surprising, therefore, to find Him claiming divine prerogatives, such as power to forgive sins (Mark 2.1–12), or displaying divine attributes such as power over nature (Matt. 8.27).

Then comes the great step of divine condescension. The Greek literally means, He emptied Himself. Various theories have been put forward to explain exactly what this means. One view suggests that He limited Himself to the knowledge and abilities of an ordinary man, but this is clearly not tenable in the light of His miracles and His teaching. Others suggest that He rendered Himself fallible, but, here again, this is not consistent with His claim to be the Truth (John 14.6). It surely means that Christ hid, as it were, for the time being, His intrinsic splendour or, as Weymouth puts it, 'He stripped Himself of His glory'. He took the form of a servant, literally a slave. He exemplified this when He washed His disciples' feet (John 13.1–11). Then, we are told, He was made in the likeness of men, which presumably means that He passed through boyhood and adolescence as other men have done, and had the appearance of a man because He was a true man. But, He condescended yet further—He deliberately chose to die (John

10.17–18). Logically He should not have died, since death had come into the world as a result of sin and He was sinless. Furthermore, He chose the most shameful and degrading death the world of that day knew—the death of a common criminal on a Roman gibbet.

So, in these seven steps, we see the love of God in Christ reaching down to the lowest depths for our sakes (2 Cor. **8.9**). That is not the end of the story, however, as Paul points out. This same Jesus is exalted to the right hand of God the Father. Nevertheless, the whole thrust of the passage is aimed to emphasize the need for humility; to have the mind of Christ which was summed up by Canon Guy King as a selfless mind, a serving mind, and a sacrificial mind.

18: The Path to Perfection

Hebrews 3.1–6; 5.1–10

Christ the Son is compared with Moses the servant. We are called upon to 'consider Jesus'. Christians are designated here as 'brothers in the family of God, who share a heavenly calling' (NEB). Jesus is described as God's representative among men and men's representative in the presence of God ('apostle and high priest'). In some senses Moses shared a similar ministry, yet his status was far inferior to Christ's. Moses stood in relation to God's household as a servant, whereas Christ held the position of son and heir. Just as the architect of a building is greater than the building he erects, so God the Owner, Master and Builder of the household of which Moses was part, is worthy of more honour than was Moses. Since Jesus is God's Son the same honour belongs to Him as to the Father Himself.

In the second passage the contrast is drawn between the high priests of whom Aaron was an example, and Christ, who is 'a high priest after the order of Melchizedek'. The Jewish high priest was not self-appointed, and in this he was like Christ Himself—divinely appointed to office.

In vs. 1–4, the writer outlines the qualifications for high priesthood, one of which was an ability to sympathize with those whom he represented (2). Professor F. F. Bruce points out that the Greek verb translated 'deal gently' 'denotes in general "the golden mean between indifference and mawkish sentimentality"'. The writer then turns to consider Christ's qualifications for high priesthood. He certainly had to a marked degree the ability to sympathize with His people. In His incarnation He laid aside the dignity and majesty of His Godhead, and for man's sake, as man, He won for us the right of free access to God.

Christ's office as high priest is typified in the king-priest Melchizedek, mentioned first in Gen. 14.18. He met Abraham returning from battle and refreshed him with bread and wine and blessed him. Nothing is said about Melchizedek's ancestry—he appears as a priest in his own right, and not by virtue of physical descent. So our Lord was named by God a high priest after the order of Melchizedek—the Aaronic priesthood had been passed by.

The key verse in this passage is v. 8. The writer has been concerned with the priestly office of Christ and here he tells us what true priesthood involves. His loving obedience to the Father took Him all the way to Calvary. We cannot escape from the fact that obedience may sometimes for us also involve suffering.

19: Patience under Provocation

1 Peter 2.18–25

Peter is instructing Christian slaves to be submissive to their masters, even though they may find themselves cruelly treated at times. They have an example of innocent suffering in Christ Himself, and as His followers they should walk in His steps.

Parts of this passage are reminiscent of Isa. 53. We are reminded of the sufferings of Christ and of how He reacted to them. We are also reminded that He was the sinless One and His sufferings were for our sins.

Commenting on v. 24, Alan Stibbs points out that the statement made here 'confirms the two ideas that the suffering He endured was the penalty due to sin, but that the sins whose penalty He thus bore were not His own but ours. He thus took the place of sinners, and in their stead bore the punishment due to their sin'. In the Old Testament the expression, 'to bear sin', means to be answerable for it, and to endure its penalty.

It is interesting that the expression 'Shepherd and Guardian' is applied to our Lord in v. 25. He is, indeed, the Good Shepherd, who gives His life for the sheep. The word, Guardian, could equally well be translated, Bishop (as AV (KJV)), and, in fact, describes the function of the shepherd, that is, to be an overseer, to show pastoral care for the flock. The Shepherd who died is alive for ever more to take care of the interests of His sheep.

The main thrust of this passage concerns suffering. Christians are called upon not only to suffer, but to do so in the same spirit of patient endurance which Christ Himself displayed. Attention is particularly focused upon Christ's self-control in speech. When we suffer unjustly, it is so often through what we say that we reveal our reactions. Even under extreme provocation our Lord either remained completely silent or spoke with candour and not rancour. None of us can react in this way without the controlling power of the Holy Spirit. We need to learn from Christ that when we are being unfairly or harshly treated, we may remain calm and serene if we commit ourselves, our cause and our persecutors to God.

In v. 25 the contrast between the former condition of Peter's readers and their present condition is clearly portrayed. The straying sheep have been brought back to the true Shepherd, who loves them and watches over them as a faithful guardian.

A Christian who finds himself working for an unreasonable employer and who is ridiculed for his faith may find this passage speaks to him, both by way of warning and encouragement.

Questions and themes for study and discussion on Studies 11–19

1. As Jesus was commencing His public ministry He faced fierce temptations. How far do His temptations reveal the subtlety of Satan?
2. Our Lord came into conflict with the Pharisees over the Sabbath question. What may we learn here about how to deal with similar controversial issues?
3. What is the basic difference between worldly greatness and spiritual greatness?
4. What are the hallmarks of the Good Shepherd?
5. From John 17 pick out seven things which Christ claimed to have done during His earthly ministry.

CHARACTER STUDIES

20: Paul's Appeal

1 Corinthians 12.12–13.3

Patiently and wisely Paul sought to guide, to teach and to advise. With care and precision he went over all the problems and difficulties which had come to his notice, and had made his ruling. It was always his manner to turn from such detail to the deeper truths of Christ, and to the great eternal principles which underlie all true godly living. On such occasions his style takes wings. Observe the sweep of eloquence with which Rom. **8** ends (31–39). Then see ch. **12** of the same epistle conclude a section of close argument with a call to consecration and the practice of life's simplicities in a manner reminiscent of the moving chapter before us. 'Look,' says Paul, 'I will show you a higher path' (**12**.31), a 'way of sovereign excellence.'

His tone has been lofty, almost vehement, and we are hardly prepared for the lyric beauty of the chapter which now opens. Passion, strength and simplicity were the deeper qualities of Paul. They infuse the poem on love. Uneasy about the Corinthian pre-occupation with 'tongues' and spectacular 'gifts', he offers now, like a good psychologist, a path of sublimation. Tongues? 'Though my language be heaven's own,' he answers, 'without a Christlike character, I am so much senseless noise, no better than the noisy priests of Cybele or some other Asiatic mystery cult, worshipping strange gods with tom-toms, clashing brass, and mad din. I am a heathen without love.'

'And though I have the gift of interpretation, and am able to elucidate the deeper truths of the Christian faith, though I am an expert in theology (Eph. **3**.4), though I profess and appear to exercise a faith which baulks at no difficulty or challenge, and lack the gentle spirit of Christ, I am nothing.' There is no substitute. Giving of one's substance can be mere show without love, martyrdom itself mere exhibitionism, as indeed it has been known to be. Motive only counts in all sacrifice. The motive can be only one. Illustrate this truth from the Gospels. Consider the motives of Judas, John, James. What purified and exalted them in the case of the last two? Only love brings real advantage and all other advantage is worthless.

36

21: The Christian

1 Corinthians 13.4–7; James 2.1–9

Read the Corinthian passage again and again in more than one of the 30 or so available English translations. This is the picture of a man of God as he ought to be—and of Christ as He was. We shall translate as we go . . . 'Love is long-tempered and kind.' An enduring spirit is difficult to cultivate in this exasperating world of stress and tension. It is more difficult for some than others, and the first line of defence is what Homer called 'the barrier of the teeth'. It is a mark of Christ (Rom. 2.4 uses the same word) and if we would be like Him this trait should be woven with our character. Also 2 Pet. 3.9 uses the word: 'The Lord is long-tempered, not willing that any should perish.' The second part of the verse adds an active quality to the passive virtue. A cognate of the same word is used of the Lord in 1 Pet. 2.3, and of Christ's yoke in Matt. 11.30. Kindness is full of active well-doing (see Psa. 37.3) and finds no time to nurse wounded feelings.

'Love is not envious, is no braggart, is not swelled with conceit, is not unmannerly.' Envy, boasting, conceit, and discourtesy are not the marks of a Christian. Contemptible vices. Envy destroys all magnanimity as boasting precludes dignity. 'Conceit,' said Ruskin, 'may puff a man up, but cannot prop him up.' One might imagine that Ruskin had read this verse in Greek, for the verb Paul uses (for 'swelled' with conceit) is literally 'puffed up', like the frog in the fable of Aesop which sought to emulate the cow. Paul uses it several times in this letter (4.6, 19; 5.2; 8.1). It was a Corinthian vice to overestimate personal attainment.

Nor is the Christian a boor. Christians belie their name when they are brusque, unapproachable, vulgar, rude, tactless, indelicate, overbearing. Courtesy sweetens life. It opens doors to influence and Christ. The Christian makes no difference between high and low. He does not need the injunction James found it necessary to give. He is gracious to every man whatever his status, his class, his wealth.

J. H. Newman touched on that point in his fine definition of a gentleman. He wrote: 'The true gentleman carefully avoids whatever may cause a jar or a jolt in the minds of those with whom he is cast; all clashing of opinion, or collision of feeling, all restraint, or suspicion, or gloom, or resentment; his great concern being to make everyone at their ease and at home. He has his eyes on all his company; he is tender towards the bashful, gentle towards the distant, and merciful towards the absurd; he can recollect to whom he is speaking; he guards against unseasonable allusions, or topics which may irritate; he is seldom prominent in conversation, and never wearisome.' It all adds up to courtesy.

22: The Christian Again
1 Corinthians 13.5–12; Philippians 2.5–8

The searching description of the true Christian—the man of Christlike love—continues . . . 'Love is no stickler for her rights, is not sharp-tempered.' These qualities again add up to absence of self-assertive pride. The first phrase literally runs: 'Love does not seek her own things.' Two major ancient manuscripts insert a negative making the phrase mean: 'Love does not seek that which it is not entitled to.' That is common morality—or used to be. Paul used no negative. In ch. 9 he had illustrated from his own forbearance. And if the first phrase is biographical so is the second. Paul speaks of sharp-temper with a word related to the noun used of the quarrel with Barnabas (Acts 15.39)—a noun which Paul probably used in telling Luke the painful story. This is his word of self-reproach—and perhaps reconciliation? Was Barnabas dead?

'Love is not mindful of evil, does not rejoice because of wrongdoing, and shares in the joy of the truth.' The first metaphor is from accounting. It is the word used in Rom. 4.6, 8 for the 'imputation' of righteousness. Love does not keep a record of evil, noting down every deed done. It forgets, throws such rubbish of memory away. Nor is it glad when others go wrong. It has nothing of the evil quality which the Germans call 'schadenfreude' —a malicious joy in another's misfortune. The absence of an English equivalent is no indication that the vicious thing is confined to the German people.

'Love is always tolerant, always trustful, always hopeful, always patient.' This is not a prescription for making money. It is four co-ordinated blows arranged in a pattern of a,b,b,a, against cynicism and disillusionment, four heavy demands calculated to call for the ultimate of a Christian. The whole passage points an unwavering finger against comfortable adaptations of Christianity. Here is the character of the Christian—and of Christ, his Lord. It might be a salutary exercise to read this chapter every

38

day for a month, to learn its words by heart . . . It shows us ourselves, not, alas, in a mirror such as those Corinth made exquisitely in bronze, but in a portrait, a portrait of what we might be, should be, perhaps one day shall be.

*23: Paul's Conviction

1 Corinthians 15.1–32

There were those in Corinth who anticipated the speculations of certain modern 'theologies', and explained the historic truth of the rising of Christ from the dead on poetic or symbolic principles. Paul was utterly convinced of its literal truth. Watch his mind at work in this chapter, for it contains much of his character.

First, it is obvious that he had examined witnesses, and knew what contemporary Jerusalem and Galilee said of the risen Christ. In the first nine verses we have what is probably the first written record of the resurrection—unless it should finally be established from the Marcan fragment recently recovered from a Qumran cave that the first narrative of Christ's ministry narrowly antedated this epistle.

Then note the close and firmly pressed argument. We can do no better than translate vs. 12–19 quite simply: 'If then the proclamation is that Christ has risen from the dead, how do some of you say that there is no resurrection from the dead? If there is no resurrection from the dead, neither is Christ risen. If Christ be not risen, our gospel is without content, and your faith as empty. And we are proved false witnesses of God, because our testimony was that He did raise up Christ, and, if indeed the dead are not raised up, He did not raise Christ. For if the dead are not raised, I repeat, neither is Christ risen. And if Christ be not risen, your faith is useless, and you are still the sinners that you were. Those, too, who fell asleep in Christ are dead and gone. If only in this life we have faith in Christ, we are of all men most to be pitied.'

These are the words of one of the most powerfully intellectual men in the ancient world; and in the modern world, as in ancient Corinth, any who continue to profess or preach a version of the Christian faith which disregards the repeated insistence of the apostle concerning the very heart and substance of the message, can do so only on the basis of a complete rejection of the authority of the New Testament and of Paul's contribution to it. And they reject that contribution in the face of a clear and logical argument advanced by a man of first-class mind, whose whole plan and purpose of living was transformed by an over-powering conviction that a certain fact was true.

*24: Paul's Mind at Work

1 Corinthians 15.33–58; John 12.20–24

We have come to know Paul well as we have read what he did and what he said over the busy years of his ministry. He is actively remembering, as he writes, the events of his first visit to Corinth. Heard in Athens, or heard in Corinth, an apt quotation from the writer of comic drama, Menander, slips into his mind: 'Evil communications corrupt good manners.' It is one of two such quotations. 'No mean city,' applied by Paul to Tarsus, was a phrase of the dramatist Euripides applied to Athens.

But Paul remembered something else. If he went from Athens to Corinth on foot, he passed along the coast of the lovely Saronic Gulf, and on the way saw Eleusis, once the seat of a great, and not ignoble mystic cult, but now an industrial suburb of Athens. The cult of Eleusis must have interested Paul, because it is a fact that he took religious vocabulary from the 'mystery religions', and appropriated it for his exposition of the faith, while the substance of that faith remained Hebraic and Christian.

Demeter, the Earth-Mother, said the Eleusis myth, had come to Eleusis in search of her daughter Persephone, whom Pluto, god of the underworld, had kidnapped. She was kindly entertained, and on her departure gave a corn of wheat to the small son of the king, telling him that if it was put into the ground to die it would bring much fruit. The cult grew round this myth, and those who were annually initiated into the Eleusinian Mysteries were said to be 'born again' when, after secret rituals of cleansing and preparation, an ear of corn was uplifted. Paul may have seen the sculpture, now in the Archaeological Museum in Athens, which depicts the gift of the corn of wheat. He may have seen the plinth, which still lies in the ruined precinct of the temple, carved with an ear of corn.

He may also have reflected on the known, but as yet unwritten story of the Lord, who met the Greeks, and hinted to them that in the ritual of the Athenian cult, they had an inkling of vaster truth. As he writes to Corinth, these well-remembered associations flit through his mind. It is fascinating to watch that swift and comprehensive intellect at work linking circumstance and observed scenes to the complex of his faith. It is clear that he had combed Greek thought, pondered the words of Christ . . . 'To the Greeks he became as a Greek that he might win some . . .'

25: Paul the Administrator

1 Corinthians 16

It is interesting to see Paul turn from the high poetry and deep doctrine of the great chapter which has ended, to the mundane arrangements of the closing page of his epistle. 'Now about the collection . . .' he begins, and the theme is back on the solid earth of every day. The collection for the poor of Jerusalem was a project near to his heart. Jews all over the world were in the habit of sending contributions to their motherland, and it was Paul's deep desire to make sure that the Christian communities in no way fell short of their fellow Jews in such ministration. We have already seen how sadly the project failed. It was, none the less, nobly conceived.

We are more concerned here to see the swift decisiveness with which he goes to work. He sets no absurd standards. He makes no measure of duty, generosity or obligation in percentages, or in regulations borrowed from the Law or Judaistic practice. He makes no pressing and formal appeal. He would be the last man on earth to add to God's conditions for church membership, or to make it difficult for anyone to become an active Christian. His bases of giving are simple. Let it be an act of gratitude. The amount and the method are determined by the conscience of each, viewing his own resources and prosperity, in the light of God's grace.

He asks also for an escort to be provided to carry what was probably a considerable sum of hard currency to Jerusalem. We gain the first glimpse of the able administrator who appears again in the pastoral letters, busy with the framework of discipline, order and leadership in a Church soon to be menaced by the grim power of a persecuting state.

The programme next preoccupies him. Think of his rapidly formed plans in terms of lumbering galleys, mule-back, or the hard road trodden mile on weary mile with sandalled feet. Timothy was, it would seem, sent in Paul's place. Apollos had plans of his own. Some from Corinth stood firm, clear-minded, faithful. Of such was Stephanas who had committed himself to the ministry of the Word. Such too were Aquila and Priscilla, late of Corinth, now of Ephesus, whose home was invariably a church ... The faces flit and pass and we wish we could know more.

Questions and themes for study and discussion on Studies 20–25

1. Define love.
2. Are there limits to tolerance?
3. Is anger ever free from taint of sin?
4. The defence of the doctrine of Christ's resurrection today.
5. Have concepts in non-Christian religions any value?
6. What guidance on Christian giving may be truly found in the New Testament?

THE CHURCH'S MINISTRY AND ORDINANCES
The Ministry of the Whole Church

Introduction

The New Testament uses a number of different images to describe the Christian Church. Probably that of 'the Body of Christ' is one of the most significant. As Paul points out, a body 'does not consist of one member, but of many' (1 Cor. **12**.14). The overall impression of this illustration is that members of the Christian Church have varied ministries all of which are important. The New Testament does not imply that the Church should be dominated by one personality, but that the ministry should be shared by all the members. Forms of ministry may vary, but all are endowed with spiritual gifts of one kind or another which they are called upon to use to the glory of God under the direction of the Head of the Body, who is Christ Himself.

26: Spiritual Gifts

1 Corinthians 12

Although the subject of spiritual gifts is the main theme in this chapter Paul begins by reminding the Corinthian church that no one can sincerely acknowledge Jesus Christ as Lord unless and until he has been brought to that position by the illumination of the Holy Spirit. All true Christians have, by various roads, been brought to acknowledge Him as such, and this fact in itself gives them a basic unity.

Our spiritual unity in Christ is, however, a unity in diversity, for not all are given the same spiritual gifts. Every Christian, however, is gifted in one way or another, even though there is enormous variety in the gifts. Some are obviously more spectacular than others, and Christians are encouraged to covet the best gifts and not necessarily the most spectacular.

Paul makes clear who the Giver of these spiritual gifts is and why they are given. The bestowal of gifts lies within the sovereignty of God (11). Yet, underlying all the gifts is one basic purpose—

they are to be exercised 'for the common good' (7). In other words, any thought of self-display or exhibitionism is ruled out. There are in the New Testament several different lists of spiritual gifts, none of which is necessarily complete in itself. In this chapter there are, in fact, two such lists. Some Christians who find it difficult to recognize themselves as having any of the gifts mentioned may all too easily have overlooked the word 'helpers' (28). There are in the Christian Church many opportunities for service for those who are prepared to lend a helping hand, but who may never have the limelight.

Paul pictures the various members of the Church in terms of the constituent parts of a human body. All the various parts have a function to perform and belong together, even though their functions are vastly different. Some church members who are less obviously gifted than others may be inclined to develop an inferiority complex, but this is dishonouring to God. Others with some spectacular gifts may tend to adopt the air of superiority, disparaging their fellow members who do not have such spectacular gifts. This is equally dishonouring to God, since each is responsible to accept gratefully the gift he has been given, and to use it to God's glory. Christians within the Body of Christ are interdependent, and not independent.

27: Spiritual Unity

Ephesians 4.1–16

Paul's letter to the Ephesians has more to say than any other about the Church. The apostle speaks of the basic unity which believers have in Christ, enumerating some of the points on which they are essentially one. Because potentially this unity already exists, this does not mean that we may take it for granted. Christians are still human, and have very 'rough edges'. If our God-given unity is to be preserved and enjoyed, we must work at it, and this involves showing lowliness, meekness, patience and loving forbearance (2). Note that the apostle does not call upon his readers to manufacture spiritual unity, but rather to maintain it (3). There is a constant danger, especially in the modern world, that men should sometimes, for reasons of expediency, try to create a spiritual unity which is not of the Spirit's making.

There is a close parallel between vs. 7–12 and a similar list of spiritual gifts in 1 Cor. **12.** In neither case does Paul give a complete list, but merely points out that these are gifts of the ascended Lord, and every individual believer is included in the distribution. Furthermore, they are gifts with a purpose—they are given to equip the people of God for effective ministry (12).

Gifts, then, are not an entity in themselves, nor should they become a preoccupation with us. Rather, the ultimate goal of Christian grace is spiritual maturity, described here as 'the measure of the stature of the fullness of Christ.' In other words, a mature Christian is essentially Christlike whatever spiritual gifts he may or may not have. In the process of growing up spiritually we may have our ups and downs and sometimes be tossed to and fro, but as we grow in grace and become more settled in our convictions we should find ourselves more ready to fit in with our fellow Christians within the Body under the Headship of Christ Himself.

Unity is not to be identified with uniformity. Members of the Church are like the members of a human body—they have different functions to perform. In order to fulfil such functions God's people are equipped with a wide variety of spiritual gifts. By the faithful use of these gifts the Church is built up. Christians should grow both in love and unity. In an age when organizational unity tends to be so greatly emphasized, it is salutary to remember that the unity which the New Testament envisages is essentially 'the unity of the faith'. Truth and love are not to be mutually exclusive. We should not neglect truth when we strive for unity.

28: Spiritual Responsibilities

Hebrews 3.12, 13; 10.23–25; 12.12–17

In each of these passages stress is laid upon the responsibility which Christians have for one another. There is always the danger, even in the life of a Christian, of 'falling away from the living God', and, for this reason, we owe it to one another to be mutual encouragers. An isolated Christian is more likely to succumb to the temptation to backslide than one who is regularly in contact with his fellow believers. In a truly Christian fellowship the members have a sincere concern for the spiritual well-being of each one, and will instinctively seek to help one in danger of slipping away.

In the second passage the thought is much the same. Here again, there is the implication that we can waver and lose out spiritually, and we need the kind of provocation which comes from contact with fellow Christians. It is a pity that the word is normally used in an unfavourable sense. The meaning here is that Christians should stimulate one another to be more loving and more involved in good works. The dangers of Christians hiving off and withdrawing from the local fellowship are envisaged here. None of us can ever be a loner, particularly in the light of the days in which we are living. We need the help and encouragement that come from Christian fellowship.

In the third passage the call to be encouragers to those who are discouraged is sounded once more. The exhortation here is couched in Old Testament language without being a direct quotation. As so often in the letter to the Hebrews, the danger of falling away is shown to be very real, and so Christians must be on their guard not only so far as their own lives are concerned, but also on behalf of other members of the fellowship. As Professor F. F. Bruce comments, 'If some incipient sin manifests itself in their midst, it must be eradicated at once; if it is tolerated, this is a sure way of falling short of God's grace, for the whole community will then be contaminated.'

In times of spiritual dearth and moral declension Christians have a special responsibility towards one another. The strong should help the weak. In a materialistic age we need particularly to guard against the folly of Esau who, 'sold his birthright for a single meal'. Christians have a duty to remind one another continually where their priorities lie.

29: Varied Ministries

1 Peter 4.7–11

In this passage Peter is dealing with some of the practical demands of Christian discipleship. Christians are to live in the light of the impending return of Christ. Since time will soon be at an end we should live now in the full enjoyment of God's varied gifts of grace. Love, above everything else, is to be the hallmark of God's children. Christians are consistently called upon to regard love as their top priority, since it is through this that they make their distinct witness to the world (John 13.35). One expression of this love, particularly emphasized in the early Church, was the showing of hospitality to Christians from other places. The implication here is that such hospitality was frequently called for and should be displayed without any sense of resentment.

As in other New Testament passages, it is assumed that Christians enjoy a variety of spiritual gifts by the grace of God. These are to be used to His glory and not to be disregarded. A Christian is a steward of such gifts as are entrusted to him. There is no suggestion here that spiritual gifts are confined to one or two leaders in the local Christian community. The gifts vary considerably—some are to minister through teaching and preaching, while others will be enabled to serve the Lord through acts of practical kindness. Those who speak must do so with a due sense of the solemnity of the occasion, since they speak in God's name. Those who exercise a ministry along practical lines should be ready to recognize the divine source of the abilities which they have been given. Whatever form our Christian service may take, the aim and object of it should be the glory of God.

In this passage the most significant phrase is 'good stewards of God's varied grace'. This underlines the fact that all the endowments we may have we hold in trust, and, furthermore, it shows that our forms of ministry may vary considerably. It is a great mistake to imagine that we are all called to the same kind of service. We should neither envy nor despise those who have gifts that differ from our own. As Paul points out elsewhere, God in any case is sovereign in the bestowal of such gifts (1 Cor. 12.11).

Probably one of the hardest lessons to learn is how to respect individuality and at the same time preserve unity. The plan of God for His people is that they should enjoy 'diversity in unity'. We must avoid the temptation of trying to cast everyone in the same mould.

Questions for further study and discussion on Studies 26–29

1. How would you describe a spiritual gift? (1 Cor. 12).
2. Point out some of the defects in character which militate against the enjoyment of spiritual unity (Eph. 4).
3. What should our attitude be towards those facing special trials? (Heb. 12.12–17).

CHARACTER STUDIES

30: Paul's Pain

2 Corinthians 1 and 2

No document in the New Testament is so full of tantalizing questions as the second letter to the Corinthians. We are left to conjecture so much. A large tract of events has escaped our knowledge and scrutiny, and we can do no more than guess at the strained relations between Paul and Corinth, and wonder whether an unrecorded visit was behind some of his pain, and what, at last, was the outcome.

Another visit, in the existing state of tension, was evidently ruled out (2.1), but Titus was sent, and so anxious was Paul over the unsatisfactory conditions in Corinth that he went as far as Macedonia to hear more quickly his personal report. The whole letter is full of Paul's personality, his character breathes in every line, and although we must resign ourselves to ignorance on much of the Corinthian story which we should be glad to know, it is worth reading the letter through with care in order to understand better the loving, anxious, yearning man who wrote it in much agony of mind.

Paul was worried. That was no blemish on his faith. 'Some people,' wrote C. S. Lewis, 'feel guilty about their anxieties and regard them as a defect of faith. I don't agree at all. They are afflictions, not sins. Like all afflictions, they are, if we can so take them, our share in the Passion of Christ.' This is what Paul said (1.5).

Apart from the anxiety and stress which the isthmus church had inflicted on him, Paul had recently faced some dire danger. No one knows what it was. Perhaps it was a bout of the malady which periodically afflicted him (12.7–9). It could have been some form of persecution. Whatever it was, it remains a mystery as obscure as the act of indiscipline on the part of some member of the difficult Corinthian congregation, and it was a wound salted and chafed by the attack upon his reputation which seems to have taken place.

What is notable in these two chapters is the very matter of our quest—the character of the writer, tender with those who had deliberately or thoughtlessly hurt him, concerned even with the chief offender, lest he suffer unduly for his sin, anxious not to say a word too much in condemnation, but exalting Christ in all his sufferings. Joy flashes through his pain, for Paul lived in the conviction that he walked no untrodden path, even in the valley of the shadow. One had gone before—to Gethsemane and the Cross.

31: Titus

2 Corinthians 2.12–17; 8.1–6; Galatians 2.1–3

Titus is not mentioned in Acts, but was obviously a trusted helper and messenger of Paul. He went with Paul and Barnabas to the Jerusalem conference mentioned in Galatians (2.1). He was a Gentile, but was not compelled to undergo the Jewish rite. He had a large responsibility in the troubled period in Corinth, and came to report progress to Paul with major parts of the task unfinished, for Paul wanted him to return. Titus must have been a man of great diplomatic gifts and notable tact to undertake this difficult and delicate task. One might therefore imagine that he was Timothy's senior, and nearer middle age than youth. He might also have been the stronger personality of the two aides.

A comparison of references in chapters 2 and 7 of this letter, suggests that Titus carried to Corinth a communication which has not survived (called 'a severe letter'). In 7.6 we read that he was able to tell Paul in Macedonia some good news about the troubled congregation. They probably met in Philippi. It was in consequence of this Corinthian assurance, that the letter before us was written and carried off to Corinth (8.16,17) with some eagerness. This fact would suggest that he was deeply involved with the Corinthian congregation, and glad to carry a token of reconciliation. In 8.23 Paul speaks warmly of Titus as his 'partner and fellow helper'.

The remaining information is to be surmised and culled from the pastoral letter addressed to him by Paul. Titus must have accompanied Paul to Crete, in the period following the apostle's release from his first confinement in Rome. A church was founded among the islanders, and Titus was left there to organize it and consolidate it—another position of considerable trust and responsibility.

Titus was then asked to join Paul in Nicopolis, when either Artemas or Tychicus arrived in Crete to take over from him, and it is conjectured that he was despatched from Nicopolis to evangelize the towns of Dalmatia (2 Tim. 4.10). Later tradition speaks of his returning to Crete and living out his long life as the leader of the Christians there. It is also surmised that he might have been Luke's brother, which would, at least, account for his omission from the story in Acts. We follow the movements of a good man, but fail to see his face or to know him. He was most obviously faithful and true.

32: Paul's Courage

2 Corinthians 4

This is a valiant chapter. Paul knew the body's weakness. He knew the power of anxiety. He was no stranger to the assaults which evil presses home upon the mind. He knew the weight of the Enemy's attack. Often he felt like Alfred in Chesterton's poem, which we have quoted before—

> *With foemen leaning on his shield*
> *And roaring on him when he reeled . . .*

His shield was faith, and he crouched behind it, though the arrows and the slingstones clanged.

He preached, he says, a plain gospel with no subtle devices of persuasion, no concealing of all that faith involved. 'I use no crafty tricks, no dishonest distortions of the Word of God,' he says (2), 'I state the truth with clarity, setting myself before the honest judgement of the world at large.' He was no sophist, no popularity-hunting charlatan, no sly deceiver. And if the gospel was obscure to any who heard, it was obscure because of the self-inflicted blindness which is known in the modern world as well as it was in the world of Paul. There is still the 'academic mind' of the Epicurean, unable to listen to a statement which cannot be tested by a narrow range of rigid criteria. There is still the bigot, religious or irreligious, incapable of challenge or rebuke, committed in such fashion to wrong or to evil, that no thrust of truth or goodness can pierce the defence.

Verse 7 tells of weariness. Treasure was stored in pots of earthenware. In 1947 a Bedu boy threw a stone into a cliffside cave, heard the clatter of shattered earthenware, and so discovered the Dead Sea Scrolls. Paul felt a little like a fragile jar, containing such treasure—'This treasure, the glory of God in

50

Jesus Christ, is lodged in a vessel of fragile clay.' With which the old soldier rises to fight again, 'hard pressed but not beaten down, puzzled at times but never without hope' (8), 'hounded but never abandoned, struck down but never beaten' (9) ... Read the chapter carefully. Paul has had a brush with death, and realizes afresh his frail mortality. It fills him with awe to think how weak a container it is which carries the ardour of his mind, the power of his faith, the reality of Christ's indwelling. But he carries on— 'to seek, to strive, to toil and not to yield' ...

33: The Ambassador

2 Corinthians 5.14–6.10

The Epicureans believed that the gods took no thought of man, they were remote from sound or sense of human sin or sorrow. Paul served a gospel whose whole meaning was that God was intimately involved with man to the point that He revealed in Christ His character, His presence, His love, all, indeed, that the mind of man could comprehend of Him.

All that which is committed to God is transformed by His Spirit. Paul wrote much of this letter under stress, and with the 'severe' communication which has disappeared in the forefront of his mind. He sought to exalt Christ, and in the ardour of that endeavour put into inspired words the whole Christology of the New Testament: 'God was in Christ reconciling the world to Himself.' God Himself, such is the overwhelming and amazing truth, suffered in the Crucified. He was no aloof and demanding Judge, insistent on some quantum of punishment exacted from a loving Lord who stood between errant and sinful man and a wrathful Yahweh. He was Himself the Loving Lord. In the Son the Father bled. He truly bore our sins. It was the only way God could show how He was involved. Christ and He were one, in sacrifice, in agony, in love.

Searching for an image Paul saw himself as an ambassador. The ambassador, in Paul's world as in ours, was the envoy of an authority, royal or political. The envoy was sacrosanct, and his standing was generally accepted. He bore his master's message, his terms of agreement, his invitation or appeal. He spoke, not from his own authority, but from that of the one who sent him. With all the fervour of his soul, Paul begs his hearers to accept the terms of peace he carries.

As Lightfoot put it in his perceptive commentary: 'The ambassador acts, not only as an agent, but as the representative of his sovereign . . . His duty is not only to deliver a definite message, but he is obliged to watch opportunities, to study characters, to cast about for expedients, so that he may place it before his hearers in the most attractive form.'

Paul's consuming passion was to be such a man, to hide himself, to speak Christ's words, in humility to witness for another, to be not his own, but Christ's.

34: The Christian in Society

2 Corinthians 6.11–7.1; 1 John 2.15–18

The characters of Scripture, as we have often seen, were men and women of flesh and blood, caught in the net of life's circumstances. Or they were beings of the imagination, built of ideals and aspirations, like Plato's Ideal State, 'a pattern laid up in heaven'. It was a familiar thought in Paul's world. The Stoics, with whom he had much sympathy, had their Wise Man, the ideal being who always acted according to the dictates of reason.

The Book of Proverbs had several such characters. So has Paul. Here he shows the Corinthians the sort of Christians he would have desired them to be; clean, uncontaminated, separate from the godless society in which they lived. It was asking much. In the close-knit city of the ancient world, paganism was pervasive. It is becoming the same again, and the Christian boycott of evil and contaminated features of society is becoming more and more an obligation—a challenge which increasingly demands decision to cut clear from the marks of character and practice which distinguish godlessness. To hold fast to Christian values and standards, to act as a Christian in business and society, in work and in play, to converse as a Christian in the community of men, daily calls for more abstention, daily reveals a stronger distinction between those who follow Christ and honour Him, and those who own no such loyalty, or upon whom the faith sits lightly.

Verse 16 refers to the temple image which Paul used before (1 Cor. 3.17; 6.19) with the Doric temple of Apollo in mind, on the ridge above Corinth's agora. He also remembers how Manasseh brought an image into the temple of God (2 Kings 21.1–9), and how Josiah, in the glad ardour of religious revival utterly destroyed such abominations (2 Kings 23.3f.). Ezekiel 8.13–18 may also be in his thoughts. Such a demand called for much in Corinth. Could a Corinthian Christian mason decorate Aphrodite's temple? Could a Corinthian Christian butcher sell the sacrificial meat? Could a Corinthian Christian artisan attend the banquet of his trade-guild in the patron deity's temple, where worship was offered as part of the proceedings? Parallels can be found today. Do we wish to be 'characters of Scripture'? Here, at any rate, is the prefiguring of what we should be—and what Paul was.

35: Paul's Forbearance

2 Corinthians 10

There is no part of this intensely autobiographical epistle which we should be more glad to understand than this chapter. Clearly enough, some cruel and cutting words had been said about Paul in Corinth. He was bold enough when writing to them, some said, but did not dare to speak so frankly in their presence. No one could properly charge Paul with lack of courage in his public utterances. Acts is proof enough of that. They had mistaken his humility for hesitancy, his restraint for cowardice. To place an evil interpretation upon what is good was a Pharisaic sin which earned one of the Lord's most awesome words of condemnation.

They had also misinterpreted his motives. He was, they said, exalting himself. He had personal reasons for chiding them. He can only say in reply that he sought only the honour of Christ. He gently tells them that he could, if he would, assail them with all the carnal arguments they seemed to value. He preferred simplicity and the dominance of Christ. This was his theme in the gently ironical first four chapters of the first letter he wrote to them.

And then, most contemptible criticism of all, some, it would appear, had made fun of Paul's undistinguished personal appearance. The nether depths of discourtesy, dishonour and cruelty are touched by any man who taunts another with any defect, blemish or uncomeliness of person. Amid the vices which multiply in the world, there is one which seems, strangely enough, to have diminished. Even the compassionate Charles Dickens could find matter for fun in bodily peculiarities. Charles Lamb, as gentle as Dickens, describes without burning protest, the marred skin, and doomed, bloodshot eyes of a small victim of the Victorian chimney-sweep, who laughed at Lamb's misadventure in the street.

Perhaps the world today is more aware of the pathology of ugliness. Perhaps Corinth, too, lacked conscience here.

Finally, some said, he claimed an authority to which he had no right. Paul was a rabbi, had probably been a Sanhedrist and was a brilliant intellectual. That such criticism was made of him, revealed the smallness of the critic. The theme to follow in this sad record of slander and malice on the part, surely, of a Corinthian minority, is the meekness, gentleness, and forbearance of the victim. Here is one example. It was a man of surpassing faith, love and humility who could so withhold his hand.

36: Paul's Path

2 Corinthians 11

Here is another page of biography, much of which eludes us. Some of Paul's sufferings are known to us and can be aligned with details in this chapter—the stoning, for example at Lystra (Acts 14.19). The earliest date which can be assigned to the second letter to Corinth is A.D. 57 or 58, so some of the events in later chapters of Luke's narrative are to be added to this daunting list. The wreck on Malta was Paul's fourth shipwreck. We are faced with unrecorded pages of history.

Like Valiant-for-Truth in Bunyan's story, Paul had 'fought till my sword did cleave to my hand, and when they were joined together, as if a sword grew out of my arm, and when the blood ran through my fingers, then I fought with most courage.' And it was after this, says Bunyan 'that Mr. Valiant-for-Truth was taken with a summons, and had this for a token that the summons was true, that his pitcher was broken at the fountain . . . Then said he: "I am going to my Father's; and though with great difficulty I am got hither, yet now I do not repent me of all the troubles I have been at to arrive where I am. My sword I give to him that shall succeed me in my pilgrimage; and my courage and skill to him that can get it. My marks and scars I carry with me, to be a witness for me that I have fought His battles who now will be my Rewarder."'

Paul might have been the model for Bunyan's brave picture. Linger over v. 27. It gives a picture of such travel as Paul endured, no plush speeding from place to place, but travel as travel was in a world which the Romans, the first great road-builders, were only beginning to open up with their vast network of paved military highways. It was largely unpoliced, with large hinterlands filled with still dissident tribesmen. In Asia Minor, the distances still seem vast to the visitor who speeds round the sites of ancient churches with all the rapidity and ease of modern travel. What they seemed to the weary-footed missionaries of the first century, is difficult to imagine.

And consider the fact that all the stress of limb and muscle was, in Paul's mind, secondary to the burden he bore upon his spirit—the care for the souls of men, the anxiety he felt over the unceasing pull and tug of the pagan world upon the loyalty and life of those so hardly won, the fragility of many, the sabotage within, the crass betrayal. Such loads lie heavy on the soul, but they are part of the task a man undertakes who decides to be a Christian. Paul saw in it the privilege of taking up Christ's burden, sharing, in a mystic way, His sufferings. And as he did, so must we. The load of the world's pain lies on the heart.

Questions and themes for study and discussion on Studies 30–36

1. Mental persecution, slander and personal criticism in the Church.
2. The qualities of the peacemaker. What is tact?
3. The worth and limitations of the 'academic mind'.
4. The role and qualities of an ambassador.
5. Christian abstention in modern society.
6. Cruelty and humour.
7. Our debt to Paul.

THE CHURCH'S MINISTRY AND ORDINANCES

Paul's Principles of Ministry

Introduction

In 2 Corinthians we see how intimate a relationship existed between Paul the pastor and his people, the church at Corinth. Although Paul had a lowly estimate of himself (Eph. 3.8), he never belittled the ministry with which he had been entrusted, and never shrank from those aspects of it which caused him pain. He could never have been accused of seeking cheap popularity, because he realized that stewards must always be faithful and sometimes this involves administering a rebuke.

37: A Ministry of Suffering

2 Corinthians 1.1–11

The church at Corinth consisted mainly of Gentiles with little or no education—they found it difficult to keep true unity, and also to maintain a high moral tone against the background of a corrupt society. In Greek plays a Corinthian was usually pictured either as a drunkard or a prostitute. It is not surprising that Paul's converts at Corinth were a special concern to him. The church was founded during the apostle's stay of eighteen months (Acts 18.1–11). Some five or six years later it seems Paul paid a further visit, but, in the meantime, he was in correspondence with the church. It is likely that Paul wrote more than the two letters we have, including a 'painful' and severe letter which we do not possess. As he writes in this second letter the apostle is contemplating a further visit to Corinth and the letter seeks to prepare the way. In the meantime he has had a report from Titus and has been somewhat encouraged by it.

After the customary greetings and thanksgiving Paul immediately turns to the subject of suffering and testifies to the grace of God which has sustained him at times when he has been afflicted. He points out that suffering equips us for a ministry to others. The Christian is called upon to endure the same kind of suffering as Christ endured (cf. Matt. **20.23**)—although, of course, without atoning significance—but the divine comfort is always sufficient for the occasion. Speaking of his own suffering Paul says, 'we were completely overwhelmed, the burden was more than we could bear, in fact, we told ourselves that this was the end' (v. 8, J. B. Phillips). We do not know exactly the form that this suffering took, but probably the people to whom he was writing were familiar with it. It is clear that Paul had faced some extreme danger, which almost cost him his life, and which partially unnerved him—it was such that only God could deliver him, and He had done so in answer to the prayers of the Christians at Corinth. Because of what God had done for him the apostle was encouraged to believe He would continue to help him.

It is noteworthy how grateful he was for the intercession of his Christian friends. Prayer is one of the most effective means we have at our disposal for encouraging others. Christians should particularly pray for their leaders and for those involved in the thick of the battle. Christian leaders in turn should recognize how much they depend on the love, loyalty and prayerful support of their followers. Paul makes it clear that he needed the prayers of the Corinthian Christians.

38: A Faithful Minister

2 Corinthians 1.12–2.17

Paul is defending his integrity. He points out that his ministry has not been prompted by self-interest; he has not been motivated by selfish considerations; he was not a man to go back on his word; he was not one to say yes and no in the same breath any more than Jesus Christ was a 'yes' and 'no' person. Christ did not waver in His purpose, and neither should His servants.

Paul makes it clear that the purpose of his ministry is not to domineer, nor to cause unnecessary pain. He comes to his followers not as a dictator, but to be helpful and bring encouragement. Nevertheless, there must be discipline in the church. It is not stated specifically what the offence was which was then causing tension in Corinth, but there was clearly a church member who had caused the apostle grief. While Paul bore him no malice, he made it clear that he was unwilling to pay a further visit to the church until the problem had been settled. He recalled the tensions he had faced on a previous visit and he did not want a repetition of this. Since that visit he had written a letter to the offender, and possibly to the whole church, regarding his conduct, and all he sought was genuine repentance on the part of the offender. It was not only Paul who had been upset by this man's actions; the whole church had been affected (cf. 2 Cor. **2.5**). If the man were to be forgiven, then the church as a whole would have to receive him back into fellowship, and Paul urges the Corinthians to do this, lest he be 'overwhelmed by despair' (7). He should be brought back again to the Christian community and encouraged in Christian service. Paul urges them to reaffirm their love for him (8). Since God has so freely forgiven us, we must be ready to forgive others. If we fail to do so, we give Satan an advantage in the church.

In the closing verses of this chapter Paul strikes a different note. He expresses his jubilation as being comparable to the triumph of a Roman general. When a conqueror returned from battle he was often given the privilege of marching his victorious troops through the city of Rome. Special sacrifices were offered in his honour and the air was heavy with the odour of incense. To the victorious soldiers the incense was an odour of life for they were sharing in the spoils of victory. To the unfortunate victims chained to the wheels of the chariots the incense was the odour of death, for they would be facing execution. Paul and his colleagues were 'a sweet savour of Christ' (15), but to those who refuse the gospel they were a savour of death. Paul ends this passage by underlining the sincerity of his ministry. He spoke from his heart, and did not seek to make capital out of his preaching. He spoke as from God and in his ministry there was no trace of professionalism.

39: A Minister of the New Covenant

2 Corinthians 3

In this passage the apostle raises the question of testimonials. He is not particularly interested in references as such. His converts were themselves a testimony to the genuineness of his missionary activity. The only Bible the world reads is written on the lives of Christian people. Paul's confidence was not in himself—he was but the instrument which God had used. By the grace of God alone he was what he was.

Paul saw himself as a minister of the New Covenant inaugurated by Christ on Calvary. This was essentially a spiritual covenant to be proclaimed by men who had been quickened by the

Spirit. The letter of the Old Covenant served to condemn men, while the Spirit under the New Covenant communicates life. Herein lies the essential difference between the law and the gospel. Although the law given through Moses condemned, it had a necessary function in the education of man's moral sense. Furthermore, it reflected the character and purpose of God. The greater glory of the New Covenant, however, lay in its superior function. Under the Old Covenant man was convicted of sin, and was condemned; under the New he is made right with God. The difference is between condemnation and righteousness. The splendour of the Old Covenant is eclipsed by the glory of the New, so much so that by comparison the Old hardly appears glorious at all (10). Because he is living under the New Covenant Paul is confident, courageous and outspoken. Moses had to veil his face to hide the fading glory but now it is different. Whenever a Jew turns to the Lord and sees in Him the perfect fulfilment of the Mosaic Law, the veil is removed. Paul goes on to speak of the transformation taking place daily in the lives of those who are indwelt by the Holy Spirit. This transformation comes about when the believer contemplates the glory of God in the face of Jesus Christ, and is essentially a spiritual transformation. The Christian life is progressive in that the disciple becomes more and more like his Master. There is a sense in which we are already saved; another sense in which we are being saved, and yet another sense in which we are yet to be fully saved.

In v. 6 Paul has condensed into a brief sentence New Testament teaching about the law and the gospel. He expounds this more fully in Rom. 7 and 8. It is tragic when Christians, who should be living in the light of the New Covenant and the freedom which it brings, lapse into legalism. As one commentator has put it, 'When the sun has risen, the lamps cease to be of use'. This is an overstatement but the point is clearly made. As Christians we have not been brought into bondage to a new set of laws, but through a changed heart we have been made into new men.

40: A Christ-centred Ministry
2 Corinthians 4

The fact of having been entrusted with the task of proclaiming the gospel precludes faintheartedness. Such a ministry is an undeserved and gracious gift of God. There is no room for 'disgraceful underhanded ways' (2). Paul's methods were always open and above-board—he did not act like the double-dealing politician or unscrupulous salesman. He did not dilute the Word of God in order to be popular, but presented the truth directly and faithfully.

A preacher's task is to draw attention not to himself, but to Christ—the only one who has a right to the believer's total allegiance. Paul was a preacher because of what God had done for him through Christ, and he longed to pass this on to others.

There is a contrast between the message and the messenger. The treasure of the gospel has been entrusted to men subject to human frailty (7). Paul speaks of the circumstances in which he often finds himself, but testifies to the strength given to him to meet such situations. He may be 'hemmed in on every side' but is not immobilized. Paul took his life in his hands—but a supernatural power, the very life of Jesus, was being manifested in him. His sufferings were a source of life to those to whom he ministered. Paul simply could not abandon the ministry of the Word. Everyone who himself has faith has a witness to bear to God (cf. Psa. 116.10).

For the apostle even the prospect of death held no terrors. His real objective was the eternal welfare of his converts. He does not 'lose heart' although his sufferings are exhausting—his body may show signs of wear, but his inner nature is constantly renewed. In the light of heaven's glory, passing afflictions pale into insignificance. The afflictions are transient, but his inheritance in heaven is unfading.

We cannot but marvel at the lowly estimate Paul had of himself —'a common, clay pot'—but he also knew he was 'a chosen vessel' (Acts 9.15), and he never belittled the ministry with which he had been entrusted. He never ceased to wonder at God's grace in saving him and commissioning him. It is still true that God's saving truth is entrusted to very ordinary people—people like ourselves; common 'earthenware jars', as it were.

It is a battle in which we are engaged. Yet there is no reason to lose heart. As J. B. Phillips has rendered it, we may be 'knocked down but not knocked out'. The Christian refuses to give way to despair. Christ's words about the corn of wheat falling into the ground and dying (John 12.24) are applicable to Christian service, but the follower of Christ is concerned with that fruitfulness which will bring glory to God.

41: A Ministry of Reconciliation

2 Corinthians 5

Paul is conscious of his failing faculties and the imminence of death—our human bodies are only temporary structures; they are as vulnerable to wear and tear and decay as a tent. The apostle looks forward to his eternal shelter—his resurrection body. He thinks of his spiritual body as a garment to be put on, and longs for the more permanent dwelling which will be his after death.

Paul's intense desire is to enjoy the protection of an imperishable heavenly shelter, but this does not mean he has a fanatical desire to be rid of his present human body. For the time being he is in this tent, but he desires to be better clothed to enjoy the fuller life of heaven.

He speaks of the Holy Spirit as being the 'guarantee' of future blessing. We are, therefore, to be 'of good courage' because of the Holy Spirit's indwelling presence. While the Christian is already 'in Christ' he is not yet 'with Christ'. Nevertheless, our aim, come life, come death, should always be to please our Lord (9). We must all appear before the *bema*—the judgement seat of Christ.

Paul was deeply conscious of his accountability to Christ. He was fearful of letting Him down, of being a disappointment in the eyes of the One who had done so much for him. As Christians we are not in danger of the judgement of the 'great white throne', which results in condemnation, but our faithfulness in service will be under review. The quality of the work we do for Christ is even more important than the quantity.

Paul had in Corinth those who were only too ready to denigrate him. His followers could, however, contrast his real devotion and integrity with the supposed superiority of these rival teachers. Paul was constantly under the all-compelling constraint of Christ's love for him. As a Christian he no longer views men and women solely in the light of appearances. He knows that a true believer is in fact a new creation, fundamentally different from what he once was.

A preacher of the gospel may be properly described as an ambassador for Christ. 'An ambassador is at once a messenger and a representative. He does not speak in his own name. He does not act on his own authority. What he communicates is not his own opinions or demands, but simply what he had been told or commanded to say. But at the same time, he speaks with authority, in this case the authority of Christ Himself' (Hodge). God

61

makes His appeal to men through men. Necessary qualities in those who are ambassadors for Christ are tact, dignity, and courtesy. There must be no bludgeoning or bullying.

In this fifth chapter Paul gives us two statements which sum up the message of the gospel—'God was in Christ, reconciling the world to himself' and 'If any man is in Christ, he is a new creation'. Inevitably we are brought face to face with Christ's death, for here is the basis which makes reconciliation possible. Not only do we see the love of God revealed in a unique manner, but we find here the means whereby the law of God has been satisfied. Where this good news is believed and acted upon lives are transformed. The most dramatic and radical change is in the very motivation of life. The 'natural' man's life revolves round himself; he is motivated by self-interest, whereas the Christian's life revolves round Christ, and he lives to please Him. How desperately in the modern world we need to show men and women this new way which not only brings them into a right relationship with God, but also with one another!

*42: A Responsible Ministry

2 Corinthians 6.1–10

In this passage we see the marks of a faithful ministry. Paul has already reminded the Corinthian church of his call to be an ambassador for Christ (5.20). As such, he, and the apostles generally, are God's fellow-workers. He appeals to the Corinthians not to let the Christian message pass them by, and he underlines the urgency of his appeal by quoting from Isa. 49.8—the accepted time will not always be with us.

He goes on to stress the importance of ministers not giving unnecessary offence or bringing the ministry into disrepute—'There are people who will be glad of an excuse not to listen to the Gospel, or not to take it seriously, and they will look for such an excuse in the conduct of its ministers' (Denney). The characteristic virtue of the ministerial office should be steadfast endurance, even in the face of afflictions, hardships and frustrations. Some trials are of a general nature, but some are inflicted by others, whilst there are also trials that are self-inflicted in the cause of the gospel.

Paul goes on to refer to the spiritual graces which God enabled him to display as a minister of Christ. These included singleness of purpose and patience with people. Sometimes the apostle's reputation stood high, but at other times the opposite was true. He knew what it was both to be defamed and to be betrayed; to be treated as an impostor, and yet true; ignored by some, yet well-known to others; brought face to face with death, yet very much alive; a man to be pitied in the eyes of men generally, yet full of joy; although he was poor so far as this world's goods are concerned, yet he possessed the unsearchable riches of Christ.

In these verses Paul gives us a series of vivid contrasts between the Christian and the man of the world. In the eyes of the world the Christian is to be pitied, and yet the man of the world has no conception of the joy of the believer. A keyword here is endurance (*hupomone*). It is a difficult word to translate, but as William Barclay comments: 'It describes the ability to bear things in such a triumphant way that it transfigures them and transmutes them.'

*43: A Holy Ministry
2 Corinthians 6.11–7.3

In this passage Paul is appealing for consistency of life and true consecration to the Lord. It is essentially a personal appeal. He points out that he has spoken to them without reserve. His heart goes out to them and he asks that in return they shall feel the same affection for him.

He has some clear-cut advice regarding associations with unbelievers. There must be no permanent relationship formed because believer and unbeliever do not have a common basis in life. He is probably thinking primarily of mixed marriages, but some have applied the same teaching to business partners. Obviously there must be social contact between Christians and the non-Christian world, but as one translator has it, we should 'stop forming intimate and inconsistent relations with unbelievers'.

It is interesting to note that in this passage four different words are used to show why such a relationship is 'unequal'. The words used embody two ideas—harmony and sharing. On both these counts a close union between Christians and non-Christians is ruled out. As regards marriage, Paul's counsel is clearly addressed to those, who, as yet, have not entered a marriage contract, because elsewhere he makes it clear that Christians must uphold a relationship which already exists, unless the unbelieving partner wishes to terminate it (1 Cor. 7.12f.).

The call to Christians is to separate themselves from evil and turn fully to God. The word 'defilement' (7.1) is widely inclusive and covers, not only the outward things that all are able to see, but also the inner motivation.

Separation is not a popular doctrine among Christians today, partly because it has sometimes been construed too narrowly. Nevertheless, as Denney has said, 'There is no conception of holiness into which the idea of separation does not enter'. If we are, in fact, to be separate to God, it means by implication that we are to be separate from sin and, in some degree, from sinners. The apostle is pleading for consistency on the part of believers and also for integrity. If we are going to enjoy an intimate family relationship with God, we must recognize its implications, and, therefore, be separate from all that would grieve our Heavenly Father.

In the concluding verses of this passage Paul makes a series of claims—he has wronged no one, corrupted no one, taken advantage of no one. His hands are clean. He tells the Corinthians how full of joy he is even though he is assailed by troubles on every side. There is great comfort in knowing we have not been the means of causing others to stumble but rather have pointed them in the right direction.

44: A Ministry of Correction

2 Corinthians 7.4–16

Paul has been comforted by the news he has received from Titus of the church in Corinth. We see him here as a very sensitive minister of the gospel, who feels deeply for his people. He rejoices that they have turned back to God. Earlier, he had occasion to send them a letter, the full contents of which we are ignorant of, but which clearly had some very straight things to say to the church. He had not enjoyed writing such a letter, but he rejoices now to know that it had had the desired effect, causing much sorrow when it was read, but at the same time urging them to repentance.

Paul is an example to us of moral courage in that, although he was himself a sensitive person, he did not flinch from expressing himself strongly when occasion demanded. He could never be accused of being a man-pleaser. In this respect, he is a shining example to all who are called to the pastoral office.

In the passage before us, he draws a distinction between m___ human remorse and godly grief, which alone produces t___ repentance. He points out a number of ways in which t___ Corinthians demonstrated the genuineness of their repentanc___ They had taken sin seriously and had redressed the wrong in th___ church. They had also displayed a new and revived interest i___ spiritual things, which had replaced their indifference and apathy___

We have a pointer here to the matter of church discipline, which is often sadly lacking today. Such discipline is not to be exercised merely in the interest of the offending member, but for the good of the church as a whole. In this section we find a summing-up of the whole unhappy affair, which had caused strained relationships between Paul and the church. Confidence has now been restored. If we are eager to see greater discipline exercised in the Christian Church today may we be equally concerned that it should be administered by those who have as sensitive a spirit as the apostle.

Paul speaks of his pride in the church and we can understand what he means. His confidence has been restored and the same man who administered rebuke is now sounding forth the praise of the church. No doubt we can all think of churches that cause pain to those who minister to them, but there is a place for pride in a church fellowship, not the pride of self-glory, but the justifiable pride which acknowledges a work of grace coming to fruition in the hearts and lives of the people of God.

Questions and themes for study and discussion on Studies 37–44

1. What should be the motives of a pastor when he feels called upon to rebuke his people?
2. What is conveyed by the expression 'ambassadors for Christ'?
3. What is the apostle's attitude towards growing old?
4. How should the fact of personal accountability to God affect our lives?
5. What does Paul teach about separation from the world?

CHARACTER STUDIES

45: The Galatians

Galatians 3

In Volume 13, we accompanied Paul on his missionary journeys to Iconium and Lystra. It is most likely that it was to these southern Galatian congregations that the apostle wrote his anguished letter. He wrote probably round the year A.D. 52, after his second visit to the area, and after the determined Judaistic party had found time to follow Paul's tracks and seek to draw Christianity into the fold of Judaism. They were an active, determined group.

Paul saw with intense clarity that justification by faith, the central doctrine of his theology, and the very heart and core of Christianity, could not be powerfully or persuasively preached if the plan of salvation was also to include certain requirements of the law. What he had preached was so simple. Those who came to subvert his work, made it obscure and complex. They came, moreover, as their varied successors have done, in the name of Christ. They were the more dangerous because they appeared as Christians, speaking in the same Name, professing loyalty to Christ, along with criticism of Paul.

And, as is so commonly the case, they secured a following, which was likely to split and divide disastrously the earnest and uninstructed congregations. It must always be firmly borne in mind, as we seek to understand the thought of the early converts, that they had no New Testament. It is possible that some of the basic material, at least of Mark's Gospel, was in their hands, but this letter itself is one of the first documents of the New Testament to be written. The wonder is that the Christian communities remained as coherent and faithful as they evidently did.

But how true to human form the 'foolish Galatians' ran! Paul could only conclude that someone had 'bewitched' them, and put them under some spell which inhibited the realization of the simple doctrine so clear to his comprehensive mind. Paul had done no more than uncover in his Galatian converts a characteristic of human nature. In one way or another, man seeks to add to the requirements of the gospel—to insist on some act of initiation, to prescribe some specific form of procedure, to

demand some work of the hands, some human contribution to the 'finished work' of Calvary, to exact some promise, sometimes even in cash contribution ... It panders to human pride to feel that man may make some small addition of his own to what has been done in overwhelming completeness for his redemption. The Galatian folly has been repeated in sect and individual, in the name of institution, hierarchy, cult of leadership or heresy. 'Foolish Galatians' ...

46: The Ephesians

Ephesians 2

Although we know none of the Ephesian church personally in the fashion of the Corinthian and Roman Christians whose names have found their way into the records of the New Testament, we do encounter the Ephesians in many different ways. In Acts 19 there was a striking picture of religious revival in the pagan, superstition-ridden city, culminating in a highly emotional demonstration, which ended Paul's ministry in the city of the powerful Artemis cult.

The Asiarchs, not at all displeased at any undermining of the cult, had advised Paul to leave Ephesus, but had as clearly hinted that it might be unwise to return. Hence the meeting of the elders on the Miletus beach (Acts 20), and some urgent warnings of Paul about dissensions to come in the congregation. These events covered four or five years, from the beginning of Paul's ministry in the city. Chronology is not certain to within a year or two, but say that we are speaking of A.D. 56, 57 to 58, 59.

The letter to the Ephesians in the New Testament is a theological treatise as well as a pastoral. It may have been circulated round the other Asian cities as far into Asia Minor as Laodicea, so it cannot be said that we gain much knowledge of the Ephesian Christians from it. Paul seems to have been in his house imprisonment in Rome. He is 'the prisoner of Christ'. At any rate it seems possible that the letter, like the first epistle to Timothy, was a work of the early sixties.

Soon after, John wrote his Apocalypse with a letter to Ephesus which we shall look at in a later study. The date again eludes us. The second letter to Timothy was certainly written during Paul's last imprisonment, and at a time not far from his death. This, we have conjectured, may have been in the vicinity of A.D. 67.

It is, in consequence, difficult to see the Ephesian Christians with the sharp clarity with which we were able to see those of Corinth. They would be a mixed multitude. The worship of Artemis was built upon an ancient Anatolian cult, but had been Hellenized by the Greeks who had founded most of the cities in Asia Minor, and especially the Province of Asia, during the great age of Ionian colonization. Hence, along with the Jews, a strong Greek element.

We shall gain a slightly more intimate glimpse of the baser types in the congregation when we examine some of the advice given to Timothy, who had the difficult task of managing the church, and also in the more cryptic phrases of the letter John wrote from Patmos. Paul's letter should be read right through. It is a noble utterance. He calls for faith, for a clear view of faith's all-sufficiency, for stability amid the gusts of false doctrine (4.14), for strong loyalty, for love, for ethical standards commensurate with all—but what congregation is above such exhortation? Perhaps the Ephesians were like any group in just such a pagan environment; violent, sex-ridden, torn by sect, faction, social stress—and 'standing in the need of prayer.'

47: Strong Man Armed

Ephesians 6

Paul learned much about the Empire in his journeys through the eastern and middle Mediterranean world. He knew how precariously those far-flung frontiers were held. He had spoken long and intimately with the legionaries of Rome, men who had seen the Rhine and the Danube, had served in Britain, and who were aware, as every easterner among Rome's citizens was aware, of the great, perilous open gate through which a Parthian invasion could come.

Vast pressures from the European and Asian hinterlands bore upon the frontiers of the Empire, and the soldiers who held those borderlands had the gate of Rome in their hands in more ways than one. And Paul's evangelism was, as we have so often seen, imperial in its strategy. He knew that forces of evil pressed hard upon the Church, evil which had a planning Mind behind it, and who, amid the mounting pressures of 'spiritual wickedness' in our own place and time, can deny the logic of such belief?

Let us, then, stand fast, says Paul, equally to Ephesus, to his own century, and us. He took a metaphor as old as Abraham (Gen. **15.**1), and built it into the picture of a soldier of Christ, girt about with truth. The belt of the soldier held the breastplate firm, made a place to sling the sword, and girded the loins. The breastplate, so dependent upon the belt, as righteousness is on truth, guarded the vitals of life. No true religion can subsist on lies or on unrighteousness. Integrity and utter honesty must ever be the front the warrior of Christ presents to the world.

Above all, the shield must cover the body, held high, with the helmeted head held low, that helm and targe may fend off the blows of evil. The Roman soldier could use his bossed shield offensively as well as defensively, to throw an enemy off balance as he attacked with his short Thracian sword. He could stand with his cohort, shields locked overhead in a 'tortoise', so that a roof could cover a commando on attack. To lose the shield, in Greece and Rome, was ultimate military disgrace. 'The Greeks had a word for it'—*leipsaspia*—leaving the shield behind. The helmet covered the seat of thought, the head, as the consciousness of a Saviour-God keeps thought steady, safe from shattering blows, inviolate.

The sword, two-edged, sharp, is the Word, the soldier's essential weapon. Let it be blunted, bent, made useless by the arm's weakness or inexpertise, and the soldier can expect no victory. Paul knew the praetorians well. He saw them at weapon practice, medallions glittering on their belts, breastplates shining, helmet and plumed crest down ... He saw another soldier, steadfast, disciplined, one of a legion, conquering ...

48: Tychicus

Acts 20.4; Ephesians 6.21; Colossians 4.7; 2 Timothy 4.12; Titus 3.12

Tychicus, described by Paul as a beloved brother and fellow-servant, and as a faithful minister of the Lord, was the bearer of the letter to the Ephesians, and, in company with Onesimus the returning slave, also the bearer of the letter to Colossae. Probably the gracious note to Philemon, covering Onesimus' return, travelled in the same mailbag, for it is reasonable to assume that Philemon lived at Colossae. Paul intended to make a visit to this area in the likely event of his discharge from his Roman custody, and some identity of phraseology between the two major letters is no matter of importance. Paul also intended the message to be made known in Laodicea. Ephesus was the mother church of the cluster of Christian congregations in the Lycus valley. There was probably another congregation in Aphrodisias, a city unmentioned in any ancient text, and only recently located and excavated. Archaeology may have some surprises there, as the work proceeds.

Tychicus is mentioned by Luke, along with Trophimus, as an Asian citizen, who met Paul in Greece and accompanied him to Troas at the conclusion of the third of Paul's journeys. He is not mentioned again in Acts, but is probably contained in the pronoun 'we', used of the party who travelled on with Paul. If the references above are followed in this scattered biography, it appears that Paul gave Tychicus a task in Ephesus, a natural appointment for a native of the province of Asia. He later seems to have replaced Titus in Crete. It is also suggested that Tychicus was the unnamed 'brother' of 2 Cor. 8.22. Tradition, at this point takes over, names Tychicus as Bishop of Colophon, and mentions final martyrdom. Of this there is no certain knowledge.

We have, then, a man who is little more than a name. He moves in and out of the story, casually mentioned, but whenever he appears, busy with some useful task. To carry mail from Rome to Colossae was no mean achievement, an arduous journey of five or six weeks' travel, in three peninsulas, and over two seas. Tychicus is a type of many faithful men and women, who without fanfare or prominence, carry on the work of Christ. The Church cannot do without them. They are the strength of its being.

Questions and themes for study and discussion on Studies 45–48

1. The Galatian folly today.
2. The problems of Ephesus today.
3. 'Without truth there can be no other virtue' (Sir Walter Scott).
4. The ministry of letter-writing.

THE CHURCH'S MINISTRY AND ORDINANCES

The Ministry of the Apostles

Introduction

Clearly the apostles occupied a unique position in regard to the establishment of the Christian Church. Numbered among them was Saul of Tarsus, who described himself as 'the least of the apostles, unfit to be called an apostle' (1 Cor. **15.**9), yet, nevertheless, one who was surely the greatest missionary the world has ever known.

49: The Mission of the Twelve

Matthew 10

The chapter opens with the charge given by our Lord to the twelve apostles. Matthew lists them in pairs, possibly corresponding to the groups into which they were formed when Jesus sent them out two by two (Mark **6.**7). Thaddaeus or Lebbaeus probably corresponds to the Judas mentioned by Luke (Luke **6.**16). Judas may have been his original name, which was later changed because of the stigma attached to the other Judas. Basically, the apostles were charged to go out with no reserve comforts, no second staff, no second pair of shoes, no change of clothing. When they entered into a town they were told to stay in one particular home, probably to prevent different people trying, with ulterior motives, to have a share in entertaining them. They were to use the usual Semitic greeting, 'Peace be unto you.' In cases where they were not received they were to shake the dust from their feet, no doubt as an indication that they had been staying on what was virtually heathen soil.

In their behaviour they were to be both wise and guileless. They could expect a measure of persecution, but they could depend upon words being given to them when they would be hauled before magistrates. The prospect before them was frightening in one sense, but in facing persecution and trials they were simply walking in the steps of their Master. They need not be afraid, for God's loving care would surround them and, in due time, they would have their reward. Furthermore, those who showed hospitality to them, even in the smallest degree, would be rewarded as though such hospitality had been shown to Christ Himself.

One thing that emerges from this passage is the divisive result of Christian discipleship, particularly in family relationships. There is a sense in which Christ unites, and another sense in which He divides. Even those of different races find unity in Christ, whereas members of the same family may be divided because of Him.

Disciples cannot expect to fare better than their Master. Those who go out in His name will not always find a ready acceptance, either for themselves or their message. They must be prepared to risk losing the favour of men and even face the possibility of losing life itself in the cause of Christ. The day will come however when the tables are turned, and those prepared now to confess Christ will be confessed by Him before the Father, while those who now deny Christ will similarly be denied.

The object of Christ's first coming was not to set up a millennial kingdom, but to proclaim a message which would often lead to strife and division. We must not blame the gospel for this, but the heart of fallen man. Christians cannot escape cross-bearing—to follow Christ one must be willing to deny oneself.

50: Apostolic Prerogatives

Matthew 16.13–20; John 20.19–23

Unlike the Scribes and Pharisees who had 'taken away the key of knowledge' and 'shut up the kingdom of heaven against men' (Luke 11.52; Matt. 23.13) Peter was to use the keys to open it, and he did so first to the Jews (Acts 2.38ff.), secondly to the Samaritans (Acts 8.14ff.), and then to the Gentiles (Acts 10, 11; cf. 15.7). The Reformers rightly maintained that this authority given to Simon Peter was in fact through him passed on to the Church, and was virtually a commission to proclaim the Word of God. Similarly the function of binding and loosing is not the function of an order within the Church, but of the gathered company of believers. What is essential to the validity of any binding or loosing is not the official status of those who do it but the presence and authority of Christ among them.

Some would argue that, while this prerogative was not given to Peter exclusively, it was a commission given to the apostles as a whole and confined to them.

Whether we hold to the view that this is a continuing commission given to the Church as a whole, and relating to the exercise of discipline, or was confined to the original apostles, we cannot on any count accept the suggestion that Christ had in mind here the perpetuation of a priestly caste endowed with special rights by virtue of the office held.

When it comes to the forgiving and retaining of sins (John 20.22f.) Christ's commission here clearly was one to the Church as a whole rather than to a limited group within it. It is the function of the Church as a corporate body to declare forgiveness to those who truly repent; even though the declaration may be made through the voice of certain individuals. There is no evidence in the New Testament that the apostles believed unique authority had been given to them in this connection. They could and did, however, declare authoritatively the terms on which God would forgive men's sins. It is God who forgives men through Christ; it is the Church which proclaims His forgiveness.

It is clear that the proclamation of forgiveness of sins through Christ was to be a leading feature of the apostolic commission, as it had been in our Lord's own ministry.

The giving of a key to a scribe was symbolic of bestowing authority to teach. To bind meant to make a precept an obligatory law, while to loose was tantamount to declaring a precept not binding.

As those who had received the benediction of Christ's peace and been promised the gift of the Holy Spirit, the disciples could now truly become apostles and, like their Master, exercise a ministry of reconciliation.

51: Catching Fish and Feeding Sheep

John 21

Some commentators speak of this chapter as an epilogue to the Gospel since the last verse of the previous chapter appears to conclude the narrative. The disciples, in obedience to Christ's instructions (Mark 16.7), had returned north to Galilee, but He had not yet appeared to them. Peter, restless, perplexed and nervy, says, 'I am going fishing.' It was a natural enough reaction on the part of a man whose livelihood had been in the fishing industry. There was little that you could teach Peter about the fisherman's art. Strangely enough, however, a night's fishing proved singularly unfruitful—he and his companions caught precisely nothing. Now, with the same men using the same boats success dramatically followed on failure. The Lord Himself had intervened and they had been obedient to His command. The precise figure of fish caught suggests a symbolical significance, but none of the various interpretations put forward is very convincing.

Later in the chapter we read of how the disciples accepted the Lord's invitation to have breakfast, and some have read into this account a eucharistic emphasis. After that Peter was asked three times by Jesus whether he really loved Him. Different Greek words are used and opinions are divided as to whether there is any real difference in meaning. In the first question Simon is asked whether he loves Jesus, (*agapao*) and replies by saying that he feels a real affection for Him (*phileo*), and, again, this is repeated the second time. The third time Jesus uses the same verb, asking Peter whether he has an affection for Him and receiving the assurance that this is so. Our Lord is saying, in effect, 'Are you quite sure that you have an affection for me?' This question is the preliminary to a commission to serve. Before we can enter the service of Jesus Christ we need to be sure of our motivation. Too much Christian service is done from a sense of duty, and even sometimes with a spirit of drudgery, whereas the true motivation for serving the Lord should be the constraint of divine love.

It is interesting that in this chapter we should find a reference both to catching fish and later to feeding sheep. These two metaphors are both applied in the New Testament to Christian service. When Peter and Andrew were originally called by the Lord He told them He would make them 'fishers of men' (Matt. 4.19). Now, Peter is commissioned to feed Christ's sheep, which is the privilege and responsibility of every true pastor.

Having commissioned Peter, our Lord reminded him of the costliness of discipleship. Very literally he will walk one day in his Master's steps. He is given a clear indication that he will suffer martyrdom. John Marsh comments: 'To be a disciple is not just "following Jesus"; it is to be his "fisherman", to share in his own gathering of the messianic community; it is to suffer with the

Messiah in the all-decisive messianic woes; it is to witness by life and by death, to the victory of the crucified.' One cannot but feel that we have rather lost this note and tended to glamorize the ministry, emphasizing the 'glory' of it rather than the 'suffering servant' aspect.

52: Put in Trust with the Gospel

Ephesians 3.1–13

Paul's theme here is the divine mystery which has now been revealed, and which he himself had received by special revelation. This mystery consisted in the fact that in the Christian Church there is to be a welcome on equal footing for Jew and Gentile alike. This 'Good News' Paul sees as a sacred deposit with which he has been entrusted. He never ceased to marvel that, by God's grace, he, of all people, had been commissioned to preach and to declare, to the Gentiles in particular, 'the unsearchable riches of Christ'.

In v. 8 we learn what Paul thought about himself. He invents a comparative of a superlative noun to express himself more forcefully. Here was no mock modesty. There were times when he had to vindicate his apostleship, and on such occasions he could become, as he puts it, 'a fool' in his boastful confidence (2 Cor. 11.18ff.). Nevertheless, he had no illusions about himself. True saints grow more humble as they increase in holiness. The nearer we are to God the less we shall think of ourselves. William Carey, the pioneer missionary, was invited by the Governor General of India to a dinner party. Members of the aristocracy present tended to regard missionaries with scorn. Carey overheard one army officer say loudly, 'I believe Carey was a shoemaker, was he not, before he took up the profession of a missionary?' Carey at once interposed, 'Oh no! I was only a cobbler—I could mend shoes and was not ashamed.'

Whereas Paul belittled himself he always had the highest estimate of the ministry to which God had called him. To have been put in trust with the gospel was, to him, an honour of inestimable magnitude. Paul saw himself as conveying a message which centred in the person of Christ. Salvation for him meant more than the fact of forgiveness of past sins—it related to present enjoyment of God's goodness and future glory yet to be revealed. The phrase 'the unsearchable riches of Christ' (8) is noteworthy.

Someone has commented: 'Had Paul lived, preached and written until this present day, he had not exhausted the subject, nor fully declared the unsearchable riches of Christ.' We could no doubt include among those riches His essential glory as Creator, His divine condescension, His perfect manhood, His vicarious suffering and death, His priestly intercession, His promised return and future reign. All this, and much more, was included in the full-orbed gospel the apostle Paul felt called to preach.

53: By Divine Appointment

1 Timothy 1.12–17; 2 Timothy 1.8–14

In the first of these passages the apostle Paul refers to his personal experience of the gospel, giving us an autobiographical pen picture. The very thought of being entrusted with the gospel reminded Paul afresh of his own experience of God's saving grace. As one commentator has put it, 'If Christ can change Paul, the greatest of sinners, into an apostle, there is no limit to His transforming power. So, let no man say that his duties as a Christian are beyond his abilities' (Easton).

Paul never ceases to marvel that he, of all people, should have been called into the Lord's service. He certainly did not see himself as being self-appointed, but, rather, as divinely commissioned. He knew himself to be an outstanding example of what divine grace can accomplish in a human life. The Greek word rendered 'pattern' or 'example' (16) was the word used to describe the lightning sketch of an artist. Reflecting thus on God's infinite mercy the apostle bursts forth into adoring praise of God Himself, who had saved and commissioned one who had formerly been a blasphemer and a persecutor, a ring-leader among the enemies of Christ.

In his second letter Paul again testifies to God's saving grace and keeping power. A key verse in the passage is v. 12. He commissions his spiritual son, Timothy, to guard the truth that has been entrusted to him, and at the same time warns him that Christian service may well mean suffering as, indeed, Paul himself had experienced.

Paul's personal affirmation of his faith in v. 12 is calculated to be an encouragement to Timothy. The literal rendering of the Greek here is 'my deposit'. It may be taken either as referring to what God entrusted to Paul, or what Paul entrusted to God. Dr.

Alexander Maclaren comments: 'The metaphor is a plain enough one. A man has some rich treasure. He is afraid of losing it, he is doubtful of his own power of keeping it! He looks about for some reliable person and trusted hands, and he deposits it there.' The 'day' to which Paul refers is, no doubt, the Judgement Day, the day of final account.

The apostle Paul was never happier than when he spoke of the wonder of God's saving and keeping power. He never ceased to marvel at the fact of God's grace towards him. He would have rejoiced to sing—

> *Jesu, what didst Thou find in me*
> *That Thou hast dealt so lovingly?*

For him each day was lived in the light of the coming day of reckoning. George Meredith speaks somewhere of what he calls 'the rapture of the forward view'.

Questions and themes for study and discussion on Studies 49–53

1. What principles are there in our Lord's commission to the apostles for their evangelistic work which still apply today?
2. Why is our Lord's threefold commission to Peter of particular significance?
3. What was Paul's twofold commission?

CHARACTER STUDIES

54: The Christian Citizen

Philippians 1; Luke 20.19–26

To be a citizen of Rome in the first century was no mean advantage, as the commander of the Jerusalem garrison remarked to Paul (Acts 22.28). It was in the small Macedonian town that Paul first claimed and exercised his rights as a Roman citizen. The freemen of Philippi were no doubt conscious of their standing as citizens of the Empire. Verse 27, not well translated in the RSV, refers to this coveted status. The Greek is very clear: 'One word to you, live on as citizens worthily of Christ's gospel, in order that, whether I am to come to see you, or only hear of you from afar, the news may be that you stand in one spirit, striving like a team with one accord for the faith of the gospel, dismayed in nothing by the ordered ranks ranged against you . . .'

Let the men of Philippi, says Paul, exercise their civic privileges as Christians should, in unity, with courage and without dismay. Paul is edging a little nearer in this word to the subject which disturbed him most in the news which Epaphroditus had brought from Macedonia concerning that emergence of faction and strife, with which he is determined to deal when the way has been cleared. Faction was the old curse of Greek politics. It is a malady of democracy. Where men have free speech and unfettered wills, it is inevitable, human nature being what it is, that differences of opinion will arise on matters vital to the state. In the little states of Greece, before Macedon's and then Rome's dominion imposed a unity from above, it was not always the fashion to argue and debate such differences to the peaceful end of compromise or persuasion. The Greeks invented democracy. No people had thought more constructively on the issues of politics. Few people have more impatiently thrust principles aside and reddened their history with violence and strife.

Responsibility cuts both ways. A Christian should be a better citizen of Philippi and Rome. A Roman citizen, a privileged member of a great society, should be a better Christian, balanced, respectful of others' rights, responsible. Rome and the Church were to clash. It was the Empire's great and most awful mistake, the most evil legacy of the execrable Nero. That disaster had not

78

yet come. The Christian citizen could have given Rome new life. Christian citizens are the only hope for the world's community today. Their portrait stands clear. Would they were more numerous.

*55: Paul's Impatience
Philippians 2.1–24

Paul, as the first chapter shows, had some reason to be displeased with certain elements in the Roman church, who, in spite of some admitted soundness of Christian doctrine, were taking advantage of the restrictions on Paul to undermine his authority. The Jews generally, and many Christians had shared their fate, were only just back in the capital after Claudius' decree of exile. They no doubt saw some need to walk circumspectly and with caution, a wariness with which Paul may have felt a trifle impatient (20f.).

In ch. 2 Paul seems to question the dedication of the Roman Christians, and it is a little difficult to fathom his full meaning. The true nature of Nero's government was now in full view. Two years before this letter was written, Nero had murdered his mother, Agrippina. About this time Burrus, the competent commander of the city garrison, died. He and Seneca were restraining influences on the vicious young emperor, and on Burrus' death, and almost seventy years of age, Seneca sought to withdraw from politics. City dwellers could read the signs, and may have been a little reluctant to identify themselves too closely with a state prisoner whose case had still to be decided. In another two years, the Great Fire and the ensuing persecution, made it apparent how precarious the Christians' position was.

Perhaps, too, no one was to be found in Rome ready to undertake the three weeks' journey to Philippi. Paul, utterly dedicated himself, was prone to vehemence against lesser spirits. His stern treatment of Mark was an indication of a certain intolerance against what he deemed weakness and selfishness. Imprisonment must have been trying in the heart of a Roman summer, and Paul's outburst of feeling can be ascribed to the strain under which he lived. A man of vigour, forced to depend on others, and finding those others half-hearted by his firm standards, might very naturally express himself with emphasis. The Roman church need not, therefore, at this distance be judged harshly. Congregations too often fall short of their minister's ideals. Paul likewise merits no mark of condemnation. He is the more human in our eyes for his words, and it is the fashion of Scripture to permit frank self-revelation.

*56: Epaphroditus

Philippians 2.25–30

Let us set the story in modern language for it contains its own message.

'I consider it necessary to send to you my brother Epaphroditus, my fellow-worker, and fellow-soldier, your delegate and the minister of my need. He longed for all of you, and was in great distress because you had heard that he was ill. Ill he was indeed. He almost died. But God had pity on him, and not only on him but on me, that I might not have one grief on top of another. I send him therefore the more eagerly, so that you may see him and rejoice once more, and that I may be less distressed. Receive him, then, in the Lord, with much joy, and hold such men in honour, because for the sake of Christ's work he came near to death, gambling with his life to make up the full total of your service.'

This little chapter of biography with its splendid testimonial is quite revealing both of Paul and the brave messenger from Philippi. The church probably intended him to remain in attendance on Paul, and the apostle thought it wise to leave no doubts that it was at his express command that the good man returned home. Epaphroditus had almost died in his zeal to serve. Rome in summer was an unhealthy place. August, said the poet Horace, is the month that unseals wills. The same poet describes a journey he made almost exactly a century before from Rome to Brundisium. He was accompanying Augustus' 'minister without portfolio' on a diplomatic mission. The Pontine Marshes, not drained until Mussolini's day, lay across the path, and it was the common custom to save time by abandoning the Appian Way, and traversing the marshlands by barge. Horace describes the mosquito-ridden night.

Hence Rome's indigenous malaria, to which the man from Macedonia's healthy uplands may have been a ready victim . . . It is a delightful picture, this small sketch of a devoted man who had gambled with his life for Paul's sake, and whose chief concern was lest those at home should be concerned about him. Such men are, as Paul said, rare. The RSV correctly renders v. 30. The same word is used in 1 Cor. **16**.17, which should be rendered: 'They made up for the fact that I have not you.' Epaphroditus tried to do this for the church at Philippi, and nearly broke his health.

57: Hebrew of the Hebrews

Philippians 3.1–9

Paul opens with strong words which show how intensely he feels. 'For the rest, my brethren, rejoice in the Lord ... To continue writing the same things to you is not irksome to me, while it is salutary for you. And so I say: "Watch the dogs, watch the evil doers, watch the Mutilation." For we are the Circumcision, we who worship God in spirit, and exult in Jesus Christ, and have no firm confidence in the flesh.'

The outburst is sudden. Perhaps a lapse of a day or two had brought some new experience with the Jewish deviants. They appear again later in the chapter. Or perhaps Epaphroditus, recovered and preparing to depart, had mentioned some new matter which disturbed Paul deeply.

A piece of passionately written biography follows. They, without doubt, trust in ordinances and a mere mark in the flesh, but had he not all and more than any Nicodemus, any 'ruler of the Jews'? No one had so utterly fulfilled the law, if that was all. He was of the 'chosen people', ancient in descent; he was a member of a loyal tribe, no separatist northerner; he bore the covenant sign, given on the correct day, not in the thirteenth year like some child of Ishmael (Gen. 17.25), or in adulthood like some proselyte of the synagogue. He belonged to the Jews' strictest sect, whose whole history and whose whole life was dedicated to the preservation and keeping, even to the minutest detail, of all the Mosaic Law. He had also, in the continually remembered way, fought against the Church, and had demonstrated in the act the most fanatic loyalty.

And then he had found Christ, and, in that surpassing experience, had realized that all else was trash. All his life since then, as the mystic verses which follow indicate, had been an identification with Christ. We have again and again noticed this line of thought. Paul sought to die to evil as Christ had died for evil, and to rise again, as Christ rose again, to a life utterly different. He passionately desired to imitate in personal experience the whole historic process, to the day of resurrection itself. He lived in the power of that thought, the power of the faith that Christ lives, lives in us and we in Him.

58: The Charioteer

Philippians 3.10–17; John 6.66–71

Commentators seem not to have noticed that in this passage is a word-picture of a Roman chariot race. Paul often illustrates a point by a reference to the athletic festivals of the Greeks. In this one case, writing from Rome to a Roman colony, he illustrates from the fierce and perilous sport of the Roman race. Under the encouragement of a playboy emperor, Rome, at the time of Paul's custody, was race-mad. Nero himself, as the Christians died in his gardens, after the Great Fire of A.D. 64, rode round in the colours of one of the racing factions. The common talk of the soldiers would be of racing, and Paul would gain a vivid impression of the sport.

Such a race is described well in *Ben Hur*. The charioteer stood on a small platform built on strong wheels and axle. His knees would press against a curved front wall perhaps two feet high. He bent forward at the waist with thighs flexed, and the reins were wound round his body. He leaned out, holding the reins as far forward as possible. This is what the phrase 'stretching out to the things before' must mean. The body, flung back on the reins, and braced at toe and knee, made a taut spring.

In such pose charioteer and team became one, and the charioteer was utterly dependent on his equipage. In a messenger speech in one of his plays, Euripides, the Athenian dramatist, describes the awful consequences of a fall. Ovid, the Roman poet, tells of the same disaster. The driver dared not look behind. The roaring crowd, yelling praise or taunts, the other chariots, all else had to be forgotten. A mark ahead could be the only point in the charioteer's eye . . . 'The things behind' occurs again in John 6.66: 'Many went to the things behind, and walked no longer with him.' What a picture the whole passage gives of Paul's intensity of living! So, says v. 15 with a touch of the impatience we have observed, 'is life . . . but perhaps some of you have other views— if so God will show who is correct. Meanwhile, having made a start, keep going.' So let us pray:

> *Lord make me deaf and dumb and blind*
> *To all those things which are behind;*
> *Deaf to the voice that memory brings*
> *With praise or scorn for many things,*
> *Dumb to the things my tongue could tell*

Of stumbling or of running well,
Blind to the things I still might see
When they come back to trouble me.
Forgetting all that lies behind,
Lord make me deaf and dumb and blind.
Let me forget all I have done,
'Tis through THEE, Lord, the race is won.

59: The Intruders

Philippians 3.15–21; Romans 6.1–13

The seventeenth verse can just possibly be translated: 'Become my fellow-imitators' that is, 'let us all imitate Christ.' However the enjoinder, even in its common translation, need not, indeed should not, in the light of the rest of the chapter, be taken to indicate a tone of self-righteousness. They were called upon to imitate him in striving for the goal, in abandoning the horrors of paganism, in resting all on faith, and nothing on works their hands had done.

It would appear that there was some danger in the faithful little church from some who perverted Christian liberty. Possibly the group which was a trouble in Corinth was visible, those who coalesced into a liberal faction called by John 'the Nicolaitans.' 'Ill-informed and unbalanced people,' wrote Peter (2 Pet. 3.15f. Phillips), distorted Paul's doctrine, received the gospel as a system of liberal philosophy, a scheme of emancipation which broke the bondage of old taboos, not indeed to replace them by the higher loyalties and loftier standards of Christian love, but by a libertinism which outraged the true Church. 'The Law is dead', was the motto of these antinomians, and they proceeded to make the fact an occasion for the flesh. The context of Paul's stern words in this passage illustrates a remark of James S. Stewart: '. . . there is one factor in the apostolic gospel which, even alone by itself and unaided absolutely, rebuts the antinomian charge brought against Paul and tears every criticism of the kind to shreds. The factor is union with Christ, union in His death and resurrection.'

'We should remember,' says Paul to these members of a Roman colony, 'that our real citizenship is of a spiritual realm. It has its laws, this realm, which so far transcend the laws of earth as heaven is above the world beneath. Let our thoughts be fixed there, and freedom from the taboos and restrictions of non-Christian cults simply frees the soul for loftier loyalties and deeper obligations.'

'Then, too,' he continues, linking, as always, eschatology and ethics, 'it is from that other realm that Christ will one day come, Christ for whom we wait with eager hope. Christ who will make us like Him. Such mystery is beyond us. But He who is above all and over all, He who is omnipotent, has power to transform this thing of flesh and pain into something divine and glorious.'

We cannot believe that these intruders were prominent in Philippi. It was a Roman-minded, sensible congregation. Paul was urgent to keep it so. Hence his frank warning. Hence, too, a warning which must be our next theme.

60: Two Women

Philippians 2.12–16; 4.1–7

It was a century before that, on the rolling plain of Philippi, Octavian, later to be the Emperor Augustus, had seen the army of Brutus and Cassius, assassins of Julius Caesar, driven in defeat. That was the beginning of the Pax Romana, the Roman Peace, which ended a century of strife. To be sure, there was another decade of tension which ended only with the Battle of Actium, which assured the continuation of one Rome, undivided into east and west. Augustus gave peace. Augustus restored unity. A grateful senate hung a 'civic crown' above Augustus' door on the Palatine. They gave him, till then Octavianus Caesar, his imperial name. And now Paul calls his beloved church his crown (4.1).

But through all the letter he has been working to one point. Paul had heard from Epaphroditus that two women were becoming a problem. In Macedonia women were emancipated and free. No doubt Epaphroditus stressed the fact that both of the offenders were good women. They were both right, both strong. Personalities clashed—always a problem.

Paul at last reveals his purpose. The purpose of writing his letter suddenly emerges. The tension between two women was actually the occasion for this splendid piece of exhortation, and in the light of the fact some hasty estimates of Paul's character must be revised. At first sight he appears a blunt and downright personality. Witness him expelling Mark, parting with Barnabas, withstanding Peter, defying the Sanhedrin. But if Paul is rightly read in this epistle, he has filled three chapters with winsome appeal for Christian unity, before turning suddenly, as if in some embarrassment, with one brief word of exhortation, to the two offenders. Observe, too, the shape of the verse in which he addresses the women. The names appear in alphabetical order; neither is singled out; the verb is used with both . . . Then before the two can regain breath, or recover from the stratagem of surprise arranged perhaps with Epaphroditus, the one who administered a swift rebuke is speaking generous praise. If necessary rebuke were always so handled, there would be less pain, fewer wounded spirits.

The 'true yoke-fellow' is unknown. It could have been an elder at Philippi, the originator of the complaint to Paul, whom Paul thinks it wise to restrain a little in this kindly fashion. The whole passage is not only a model of tact, but a classic pattern for managing from afar a dispute among good people.

61: The Philippians

Philippians 4; John 14.27

The Philippian Christians, for all the threat of an intruding minority, were practical folk. We have already seen some members of the church. The burghers of the town were Roman citizens, and a colony was a favoured place, and always conscious of its responsibility in the scheme of Rome's defences. The tribal menace from the north had, indeed, retreated, and the northern frontier in the Balkans was to hold for two more centuries, but Philippi, for all that, remembered that the Roman colonies were, in the phrase of Cicero, 'bulwarks of empire'. The Roman Peace was a blessing which the world prized. Rome could police the world, and so pacify the lands which clustered round the Inland Sea that Palestine no longer feared the raiding Parthians, and those who lived behind the Rhine and Danube were secure from the fierce marauding German tribes. But the Roman Peace rested on the fallible arms of men. At about the time this letter was written, London, Colchester, and St. Albans lay in ash and ruin. Under Boudicca the wild Iceni had broken out of Norfolk and struck back at Rome.

This is why Paul spoke to them of Christ's peace 'garrisoning' the soul (7). This is why he besought them to 'live as citizens worthily of Christ' (1.27)—a remark to which we shall return. It was perhaps some Roman instinct which led the folk of Philippi twice to minister to Paul's need. They are an attractive group. Of all the congregations mentioned in the New Testament, Philippi seems to have been the church to which one might belong most gladly.

Bishop Handley Moule closed his edition of Philippians in the *Cambridge Greek Testament* with the words of J. Agar Beet, and the century-old paragraph, with its touch of Victorian romanticism, and in spite of changes on the site of Philippi, is well worth quoting: 'With this reply, a gift infinitely more precious than that he brought from Philippi, Epaphroditus starts on his homeward journey. The joy caused by his return, and the effect of this wonderful letter when first read in the church at Philippi, are hidden from us. And we may almost say that with this letter the church itself passes from our view. Today, in silent meadows quiet cattle browse among the ruins which mark the site of what was once the flourishing Roman colony of Philippi, the home of the most attractive church of the apostolic age. But the name and fame and spiritual influence of that church will never pass. To myriads of men and women in every age and nation, the letter written in a dungeon at Rome and carried along the Egnatian Way by an obscure Christian messenger, has been a light divine, and a cheerful guide along the most rugged paths of life. As I watch, and myself rejoice in, the brightness of that far shining light, and glance at those silent ruins, I see fulfilled an ancient prophecy: The grass withereth, the flower fadeth: but the word of our God shall stand forever.'

Questions and themes for study and discussion on Studies 54–61

1. The role and qualities of the Christian citizen.
2. 'Congregations too often fall short of their minister's ideals.'
3. The role and qualities of Epaphroditus.
4. What was the real worth of Pharisaism? How was it corrupted?
5. The charioteer as a picture of 'committal'.
6. The Christian and compromise.
7. How to deal with tension in the church.
8. Thoughtfulness towards Christian workers.

THE CHURCH'S MINISTRY AND ORDINANCES
Spiritual Oversight and Material Concern

Introduction

While it may be difficult to establish a regular pattern of ministry throughout the New Testament there is no doubt as to the caring spirit that prevailed. Leaders in the local church were charged, not only to be concerned with the spiritual well-being of the members, but also with their material needs. Authentic Christianity is concerned for 'the whole man'.

62: The Appointment of the Seven

Acts 6.1–7

It is generally assumed that in this passage we have the origin of the office of deacon. The seven men referred to were set apart by the apostles with prayer and the laying on of hands, to assist primarily in the administrative affairs of the church, though it is clear that they also fulfilled spiritual functions. Their main task, however, was to exercise responsibility in the everyday activities of the church, while the apostles spent the majority of the time in prayer and teaching.

One has to admit that while tradition has it that the seven mentioned in Acts 6 were the original deacons, they are not designated as such in the book of Acts. Indeed it could be argued that Luke would seem to be describing a purely temporary measure to deal with a particular situation. Some have contended that the seven are in fact the forerunners not of the diaconate but of the presbyterate. A few years later we read of money collected for distribution to the poor saints in Jerusalem which was placed in the hands of men who are called elders or presbyters. Whether the seven were in fact the original deacons or not there are of course later references in the New Testament to the existence of deacons as such. It is clear, for example, that there were deacons in the church at Philippi (Phil. 1.1). In his letter to Timothy Paul sets out clearly the qualifications for those who would hold this office (1 Tim. 3.8–13).

All we can conclude with any certainty is that the deacons in the early Church represented in the first instance an auxiliary ministry, appointed at the request of the apostles to assist them. As the pattern of the Church's ministry developed somewhat they found their place in assisting the elders or bishops in the local church.

The qualifications called for in the seven are such as should mark any who hold office in the Christian Church. Of them we know virtually nothing except in the case of Philip and Stephen, both of whom did a great deal more than 'serve tables', as the next few chapters of Acts clearly show.

63: The Office of Elder

Acts 11.27–30; 14.21–23; 20.25–32

The origin of elders (or presbyters) is less clear than that of deacons. The first reference to elders is in connection with the church at Jerusalem (Acts 11.30). We neither know who they were nor how they were appointed. Some suggest they may have been the seven of Acts 6 under an official title. Others have conjectured that they were the relieving-officers for the Hebrews, just as the seven were for the Hellenists. All such speculations are incapable of proof. The only reasonable certainty is that the title was borrowed from the presbyterate of the Jewish synagogue.

There are, of course, frequent references in the Old Testament to the 'elders of the people' or the 'elders of Israel'. These men were largely responsible for the administration of Jewish communal life. They had responsibilities in both civil and ecclesiastical affairs. It was their responsibility to study the law, to expound it, and to deal with those who had broken it. Jewish elders are referred to twenty-three times in the Gospels, and eight times in the rest of the New Testament. The first Christians were almost entirely made up of Jewish men and women, and so it is a reasonable inference that they took over the office of elder from the synagogue and its administration with which they were familiar. The Greek, *presbuteros*, is the equivalent of the Hebrew *zaqen* which was the term used after the Exile for the members of the

Jewish Sanhedrin which met under the chairmanship of the Jewish high priest.

There is no reference to elders at Antioch (Acts 13.1), nor are they mentioned in the apostle's earlier letters. Paul and Barnabas, however, on their first missionary journey appointed elders in all the churches they founded (Acts 14.23). It is clear that the elders whom Paul addressed at Ephesus (Acts 20.17ff.), and those addressed in the first epistle of Peter and referred to in the epistle to Titus had a decisive place in the life of the church. They shared in the ministry of Christ towards the flock (1 Pet. 5.1–4; Acts 20.28). In the New Testament the terms *episcopos* (bishop or overseer) and *presbuteros* (presbyter or elder) appear to be interchangeable. Paul, for example, calls for the elders of the church at Ephesus (Acts 20.17), and then addresses them as bishops (*episcopoi*, 28), translated overseers in the RSV.

It is clear that the office of elder carried with it a measure of authority. An elder was responsible for leadership in the church (1 Pet. 5.1–5). At the same time he had to be careful not to lord it over the people (1 Pet. 5.3). Younger Christians were encouraged to respect the elders (1 Pet. 5.5). The duties of presbyters included teaching and preaching the Word of God (1 Tim. 5.17) and anointing the sick (Jas. 5.14). Theirs was the task of episcopal oversight of the flock of God (Acts 20.28).

64: Qualifications for Leadership

1 Timothy 3.1–13

Whereas the New Testament does not appear to give a blueprint concerning church government it does set out very clearly definite qualifications which are required in those who are to be leaders in the Christian church.

In this particular passage two offices are mentioned specifically —that of bishop or overseer, and that of deacon. In the New Testament there is no exact equivalent of the concept of a bishop as generally understood today. At least until the time of Ignatius (around A.D. 115) the word bishop was used of those who exercised oversight in the local congregation and *episkopos* would therefore perhaps be the equivalent today of minister, presiding leader, or vicar.

In examining the qualifications required in Christian leaders it is necessary to bear in mind that many church members had been converted against a background of extremely low moral standards. It was, therefore, essential that Christian leaders should be men of unquestioned moral integrity, and of blameless reputation in the local community. Qualities of temperament also come into the picture. Canon Liddon pointed out that we have here a picture of 'a man of calm, unimpassioned mind, collected, unexcitable, well composed'. Christian leaders should be those who think before they speak, and should possess sound judgement. Another essential quality is willingness to show hospitality. In the early days of the Church it was virtually impossible for a believer to accept hospitality in a pagan home. Christians as they journeyed from place to place were entertained by their fellow believers, and, of all people, the bishop must have open house. The Christian leader should not be a contentious or quarrelsome person, rubbing people up the wrong way, nor should he be a lover of money. Someone who is blatantly acquisitive is not a suitable person for leadership in the Christian church.

The qualifications for the deacon are only slightly less exacting. Those who hold office must not be tale-bearers or given to gossip; as has been pointed out: 'it is all too easy, even for Christian leaders, to become men pleasers and to accommodate their opinions to the company in which they find themselves.' It is significant that the deacon like the bishop or elder must have strong spiritual convictions. He must also be someone who has proved himself before being called upon to accept office. It is also noteworthy that one of the essential qualifications is that the leader must have the right kind of wife. A wife may make her husband ineligible for leadership if she herself is not absolutely trustworthy. She must be a true helper.

65: The Right Type of Leaders

Titus 1.5–16

The theme here is spiritual leadership in the local church. Titus has been given the responsibility for finding the right sort of leaders for the church in Crete. As in other similar passages the terms bishop (overseer) and elder appear to be used interchangeably, whereas the word steward, i.e. one who acts on behalf of another, is used of every servant of God. It is clear from the requirements set out here that Christian leadership should be entrusted to mature men of God; men of blameless character and sober judgement. They should have a well ordered family life, and be gifted with obvious spiritual grace and understanding. Furthermore, it is essential for spiritual leaders to have settled doctrinal convictions and be able to encourage and teach others.

Every church reflects the social and cultural background of its members, factors which sometimes create their own special problems. This was true of Crete whose population had the reputation of being 'liars, evil beasts, lazy gluttons' (12). Christian leaders have to understand local conditions and act accordingly. In Crete it would not always be possible to mete out 'kid glove treatment'; sometimes they would need to be rebuked sharply. The apostle goes on to point out that the all-important thing is to see that in the local church Christian profession and practice shall go hand in hand. Paul speaks in strong language of those who profess to know God, but deny Him by their deeds (16).

He uses a word that was applied to coins below standard weight—worthless. These interlopers profess to 'know God', but the way they behave shows them up in their true colours. Their stock-in-trade consists solely in their plausible language.

Against a background of moral pollution, it is essential that those chosen to hold office in the Christian Church shall be above reproach. The unfortunate reputation of the Cretans is regrettably matched by many in our modern society. The problem of false teaching infiltrating the Christian Church is not new. At Crete some of the Jewish church members were guilty of hair-splitting legalism. They probably regarded the fact that they were circumcised as a mark of superiority entitling them to be looked up to by others. Those who deceive the people of God, whoever they are, must be silenced and it is the task of church leaders to do this. When the church is threatened in this way the need for wise leadership is of paramount importance. Thus, Paul instructs Titus to see to it that well-qualified elders are appointed to every Christian community (5). Such men must themselves know where they stand and be ready to defend the faith in the face of all opposition.

66: Respect for Church Leaders

Hebrews 13.7–17

In this passage the writer speaks particularly of attitudes towards

91

Christian leaders. The reference to ruling is not in the sense of governing, but rather of teaching and guiding. The Hebrew Christians were to study carefully the lives of their leaders, especially those who had died for the faith, and were to emulate them. Whether in life or in death they had borne testimony to the unchanging Christ in whom they trusted. Just as He had met their need in the past, so He can meet present and future needs. Because Christ is changeless the truth about Him is also changeless (8), and unbiblical doctrines are to be avoided (9). These Hebrew Christians were particularly warned against the idea that one cannot become 'properly established' without partaking of special sacral or sacrificial food (Stibbs). The really important thing is to have a living, personal relationship with God, which alone can give a man peace in the midst of changing circumstances.

The Christian 'altar' is Christ's death on the Cross and, therefore, the ceremonial observances under the old covenant are no longer relevant. Those who cling to Judaism and continue in the ritual of former days are deluded and do not share the benefits of Christ's death. Loyalty to Christ, however, may involve loss of friends, and the experience of reproach. Christians have to take their place with a Christ who has been rejected (outside the camp).

In the opening of this passage the Hebrew Christians were being exhorted to remember their spiritual leaders who had passed on. Now, in v. 17 the call is to obey those spiritual leaders still in their midst. It is not enough that we esteem our past leaders, our responsibility is to submit to present spiritual guides. Christian leaders carry a weighty responsibility and are accountable for the spiritual well-being of those placed in their care. Believers are to make the work of pastors and teachers lighter rather than heavier.

67: An Exhortation to Elders

1 Peter 5.1–5

In this paragraph Peter delineates the responsibilities of elders in the local church. Primarily they are responsible for pastoral care, supervising and instructing the people of God. This they are to do under the direction of 'the chief Shepherd' Himself (4).

It is important that they should do this in the right spirit, not because they must, but because they freely choose to do so. Furthermore, their motives must be right. They are not to engage in Christian service with material gain in mind, but to serve the Lord for the sheer joy of doing so. It is equally important that their attitude should be right—they are to lead the flock, rather than drive it; to give an example rather than domineer. They must always recognize that they are ultimately answerable to the chief Shepherd, who will reward them appropriately in the last great day. One rendering of v. 5 says, 'gird on humility as an apron'. It is significant that throughout the New Testament so much emphasis is placed upon the need for humility of mind and especially on the part of those, who, because of their office, might well be tempted to show an attitude of self-assertiveness. In his lectures to students preparing for the pastoral ministry Dr. Ernest Kevan used to say, 'beware of almightiness'.

It has already been suggested that in the early Church the terms bishop, pastor and elder were used interchangeably to describe those entrusted with pastoral oversight in the local church. In this connection it is significant that the apostle Peter, far from arrogating to himself exclusive privileges and powers, is happy to associate himself with the elders as their fellow elder when he has occasion to exhort them. Then, as if to break down the mere official distinction, he goes on to exhort the younger to be subject unto the elder, and all—old and young, rich and poor, official and private—all are encouraged to 'clothe themselves with humility toward one another' (5). There is no intention in the New Testament of turning the ministry of the gospel into a clerical caste by conferring exclusive rights and privileges, indeed there are frequent warnings against the temptation to fall into any such error. The whole drift of our Lord's teaching lies in an entirely different direction.

Questions and themes for study and discussion on Studies 62–67

1. What abiding lessons are there to be learned from the way the apostles handled the situation described in Acts 6.1–7?
2. What are the most essential qualities required in a Christian leader?
3. Outline some of the main differences between ministry under the Old Covenant and under the New.

CHARACTER STUDIES

68: Epaphras of Colossae

Colossians 1.1–14; 4.1–18

Epaphras, a shortened and familiar form of Epaphroditus, was a native of Colossae and the founder of the church (1.7; 4.12), probably after being converted under Paul's ministry in Ephesus. In no part of the world was Paul's strategy of radiation more successful than in Ephesus and in the surrounding cities on the trade routes and river valleys, which ran up into the high country of Asia Minor. Epaphras was also active in nearby Laodicea and Hierapolis (4.13). This energetic Christian must be distinguished from the man of the same name (Paul does not in his case, use the contraction) who carried the monetary contribution of Philippi to Rome during Paul's first imprisonment (Phil. 2.25–30).

Epaphras of Colossae was the messenger of the Colossian church who journeyed to Rome with the disturbing news of heresy in the young congregation. He seems to have lived with Paul in the hired house in which he was under confinement, and so earned Paul's description of 'my fellow-prisoner'. This is a more likely assumption than that of actual arrest for the sake of the faith. If Colossians was written at the time of the first imprisonment, it antedated the measure of imperial repression against the Church which came only after the Neronian persecution in the summer of A.D. 64. Paul also calls Epaphras his 'fellow-servant' (1.7), no small honour, and 'a servant of Jesus Christ' (4.12), a phrase which he applies only once to Timothy (Phil. 1.1).

Such is the eminence of Paul himself that it is difficult to see clearly some of the figures around him. Epaphras must have been a man worth knowing to have done such sterling work. The Lycus valley, even greener and more fertile, and certainly more populous in the first century than it is today, was the sphere of his evangelistic activities. In the wide rolling valley plain, and very close together, lay the rich and prosperous city of Laodicea; the spa, holiday-resort and market town of Hierapolis, where the silica-laden springs attracted many visitors, and Colossae. In this triangle of towns, with their varied populace, most of them in comfortable circumstances, Epaphras exercised his successful ministry. It must have been in the Pauline mould for him to be so concerned for the integrity of the gospel. His journey to Rome is eloquent of this zeal. He must have been a man of deep concern, vast energy and faithfulness.

69: The Colossians

Colossians 1.15–2.15

There was false teaching in the church at Colossae. God was pictured as remote and aloof, ministering to men through many intermediaries; Christ was but one of these, great and effective, but not all-sufficient. Hence the superb description (1.15–23). Note the wonder of it. Thirty years before, Jesus of Nazareth, rejected and betrayed, had died on a Roman cross. And now one who had harried His early followers to death, writes of Him in terms proper to God alone. A change so glorious speaks solemnly of the reality of God's intervention in history, of Paul's own deep experience, and of the magnificence of the divine glory manifested in Jesus.

Observe Paul's method with the absurdities of the heresy which some at Colossae had accepted. What he means by saying that in Christ are stored all possible resources of wisdom and insight amounts to this: let no tamperer with the pure gospel deceive the little church into imagining that anything further is needed for salvation over and above union with Him (2.3). Let them walk worthily of that loyalty. The Christian life, commented Guy King on v.6 (where the RSV 'live' represents 'walk' in the Greek), 'is not a sedentary occupation, but a pedestrian affair'. 'Pedestrian' can be taken in two ways. It suggests a certain dogged perseverance through the common and ordinary paths of life, but it also suggests progress, a determined movement towards a goal. At any rate we must move on, not stand still. And then v. 7—rooted in Christ, let them like good trees demonstrate in the beauty of leaf, the strength of branch, and the usefulness of fruit, the deep sustenance which such roots can give (Psa. 1.3). Roots are mobile questing things. They probe and seek for sustenance, and move unerringly towards the richest supply of what they need. Let us so seek Christ.

In a tumult of metaphor, Paul seeks further to warn his flock against those who would explain away the simplicity of the gospel, render obscure that which God had made so plain, and make difficult for ordinary folk that which God had intended that a child should understand (8). Christ, he insists, is no inadequate 'go-between', but one with God Himself (9). And if that is the case, are not they who are joined to Christ by faith saved utterly, completely, triumphantly (10)? Like those who became proper Jews by the observance of the ancient rite of circumcision, so by the act of faith they became members, inalienably and eternally, of a new order (11).

It is stimulating to meet a mind so powerful, so ardent, and yet so simple.

70: The Mind of Paul

Colossians 2.16–3.11

We may sometimes almost be grateful for heresy and bent teaching, because of the magnificence of the response which it provokes. Paul's concern distils into eloquence and wealth of mystic illustration. Patiently and vividly, he has explained (2.9–15) how the Christians of Colossae became Christ's people, sharing His death and resurrection in the symbol of baptism, alive to a new and glorious life, as different from the humdrum, fear-ridden paganism around as vibrant living is from death. The great transaction, says Paul, employing yet another picture, is done. The charge against the sinner was nailed to Christ's cross, and blotted out by His blood. They were forgiven—let them grasp the fact with both hands, and realize that no more obligations lay on them. No power could daunt them, for Christ had defeated all evil.

And then we are given a glimpse of the extra-religious duties which the sectarians were seeking to foist on to the church at Colossae. There were prohibitions of meat and drink, and observances of sacred days. These, says Paul, had their place in the teaching of the Old Testament, but were not binding on Christians. Such was the teaching of those who sought to turn Christianity into a sect of Judaism.

Those referred to in v. 18 appear to have derived some strange ideas from the pagan 'mystery religions'. The 'self-abasement' may be a reference to physical ordeals and initiation ceremonies, evidence of which is found in the shrines of Mithras. The angel-worship of the next phrase touches a false doctrine already mentioned—the idea of a descending range of angel 'go-betweens' of whom Christ was only one; eminent, no doubt, but incomplete.

No, says Paul, giving us another vivid metaphor, those who are in Christ are His very body, as closely knit to Him as the limbs which move at the impulse of the head (19), alive with His own immortal life. Again, he concludes, Christianity is not a matter of rules and regulations. Those who trust Christ live not by rule but by love. In a word, the 'man in Christ' needs no irksome book of rules, no complicated and Pharisaic table of prohibitions. His conduct and his character are determined by his daily contemplation of his Lord, his daily fellowship with the risen Christ, his constant hope of being like the One who might at any moment come again. The challenge is tremendous; it forms a motive for purity of life, unselfishness of conduct, and integrity of character which by-passes all petty regulations. And here, unconsciously, Paul paints his own portrait.

71: Man in Christ

Colossians 1.24–29; Hebrews 13.12–14

Inevitably, in looking at the men and women of Colossae, and the false and foolish ideas which plagued them, we have looked into the mind of the great man who has dominated the theme for a hundred character studies. We cannot leave him speaking to the little congregation in the distant Lycus Valley, which he had never personally visited, without turning back to a strange saying which reveals much about him. It occurs in 1.24, where Paul speaks of 'completing that which is lacking in the sufferings of Christ.'

What can be 'lacking', and how can any man 'complete' such a total? Certain it is that Paul, like every writer in the New Testament, regarded the death of Christ as efficacious, sufficient, and once for all. No further sacrifice of saint or priest can provide a lacking element in that complete redemption, do anything to extend that 'finished work'. But in this world, all who associate themselves with Christ, and, in the great Pauline phrase, are 'in him', and seek to be faithful to Him in both conduct and testimony, must expect to become fellow-sharers in the same kind of treatment which Christ Himself received. Only so can Christ's body, the Church, be served and increased in number by ministry and evangelism, as Christ's followers are willing to share His reproach. This is what Paul means.

In speaking of completing what is still lacking of such suffering, Paul is thus referring to the sufferings which Christ foretold for him: 'I will show him how much he must suffer for the sake of my name' (Acts 9.16). Each day's pain, for the gospel's sake, brought him nearer to the end of his appointed course.

This is far removed, as H. M. Carson points out, from Stoicism's tight-lipped endurance. 'The Christian,' he rightly says, 'goes beyond mere endurance, and rejoices because he sees his sufferings as part of the divine purpose, and so gladly accepts them as a means of fulfilling his part in the eternal plan of God.' This is an ideal difficult to rise to, but why, in fact, are we engaged in these studies—encounters with men, some of which are dark with warning and some ablaze with daunting light? Is it not to nerve ourselves for like tasks, tasks in this case not unlike those which await our faithfulness in a not dissimilar world?

72: The Children of Light

1 Thessalonians 5

The letters in the New Testament sometimes give us tantalizing glimpses of people in the Church. It is like looking at a building from the outside, aware that it is occupied, but sensing the activity and the nature of those within by the occasional movement past a window, or by the opening and shutting of a door.

In the story of Paul's visit to the northern Greek port, we met some of the personalities of the Christian congregation (Acts 17.1–10). In the two letters Paul wrote to them we can guess what some of the rest were like. Paul, in fact, was anxious about them on more than one count. The subject of his care in Athens was the precarious state of the little group he had left behind.

He felt that he had not had time adequately to instruct them, and one theme which had given him cause for concern was the teaching of Christ's Second Advent. It is a subject which can be easily misused. The Lord Himself was clear enough on the fact that a second intrusion into history was a future historic event. He is coming again. He was also perfectly clear that it was impossible to fix the date, and that only the spiritually perceptive would read the signs aright.

It is, none the less, of the nature of man to pry into the patterns of the future. Man wants to know the shape of coming events, and every age of the Church has seen those who have chosen to disregard the Lord's clear words, and fix a date for the Second Advent. In the process they have obscured the real truth, and turned people from a blessed expectation, and in the same act corrupted some and seduced them from the proper and Christian activities which are woven into every day.

It is obvious that Thessalonica had its quota of such people. Paul warns them against such unjustified extravagance, and in his second letter is to warn them again in stronger terms. He speaks here in kindly fashion of the advantages they have. They are 'children of the light' in a real, exciting sense. They do know that the evil of a godless world is to end. They are not without hope. They need never despair. They are alive, awake, watching. It is a pleasant picture of a clever teacher leading a mistaken group of enthusiasts back to creative sobriety by extracting the good from the very texture of their error.

73: Man of Sin

2 Thessalonians 2

Sobered or puzzled by what Paul had to say about the Second Advent the Thessalonians had asked for further explanation. We can picture the more responsible members of the congregation seeking an authoritative word with which to bring some sense and order to an excitable and troublesome minority, who were distorting and misunderstanding what Paul had said.

In the process of his explanation, Paul introduces the darkest character of Scripture to be seen on earth—the man of sin, the lawless one. Paul is at pains to make it quite clear to the group at Thessalonica, who had so grievously misconstrued his words, that there were certain situations which would foreshadow the catastrophic end of 'the age'. There was to come a period of moral collapse and open rebellion against God. Some restraining power was to be withdrawn and there is still controversy regarding Paul's meaning here. Did he mean that God would cease to control evil—a statement unlikely from him? Or did he foreshadow the end of such legal protection as he had had from the Asiarchs of Ephesus (Acts 19.30f.), from Gallio (Acts 18.12–17), and from his privileged status as a citizen? Such a situation came after A.D. 64, when the mere profession of Christianity was written down as a crime against the state.

Above all the horrific incarnation of evil in a person, one destined in character, in policy, in practice to be the antithesis and opposite of Jesus Christ, would be visible among men.

Paul may have anticipated this fearsome creature in the person of an emperor, and the characteristics appeared in more than one. Indeed, as John was to remark, there were many foreshadowings of the ultimate apparition (1 John 2.18), and the world still awaits the final consummation. Some would say that there has never been a time before today when the rising flood of conscience-less evil, the growth of technology and computer science, the spread of tyrannical wickedness, and a shrinking world, have so set the stage for the second to last 'character of Scripture'. The last will be his Conqueror—Christ Himself. For us it is well to remember the lesson which Paul brought home to his misguided converts—time is not to be wasted idly anticipating an end. There is work to do, and only we to do it.

Questions and themes for study and discussion on Studies 68–73

1. The role and qualities of Epaphras.
2. The Colossian heresy today.
3. The 'man in Christ'.
4. 'The Christian goes beyond mere endurance.'
5. 'The blessed hope.' How real is it today?
6. Antichrist—the relevance of that concept today.

THE CHURCH'S MINISTRY AND ORDINANCES

Baptism

Introduction

Anyone reading the New Testament can hardly fail to see that baptism is a 'gospel sacrament'. The divine commission includes the command to baptize in the name of the triune God. The use of water as a symbol of cleansing is also beyond dispute, and generally accepted. The Christian Church is, however, sadly divided as to the subjects for and mode of baptism. The points at issue are whether the children of Christian parents are eligible for baptism, or it is to be regarded as an ordinance for believers only, and whether, in order to preserve the symbolism of the New Testament, total immersion is necessary. Over such issues there must be respect for diverse opinions, but whatever position we adopt, our understanding of the significance and importance of baptism will have much in common.

74: The Baptism of Our Lord

Luke 3.1–22

Here we are brought face to face with the preaching of John the Baptist whose ministry prepared the way for the Lord. John probably was preaching in the year A.D. 27 while the public ministry of Jesus commenced some six months later. At the time, both moral degeneration and political upheaval threatened the Roman Empire.

John the Baptist was a man of the desert and the crowds flocked out to hear him. The very way he lived convinced men he was a true prophet. Human applause and approbation meant nothing to him—he was utterly fearless in his preaching. He went right to the heart of things and presented religion in an entirely new light. He called upon his hearers to repent of their sins and to be baptized as an outward and visible sign of the genuineness of their repentance.

The truly surprising thing was that Jesus should come to

John for baptism. Understandably John was taken aback by this approach; the incongruity of it overwhelmed him. Here was the sinless Jesus seeking to undergo a baptism meant for sinners. Why, in fact, did our Lord take this step? The time for Him to begin His public ministry had arrived, and by being baptized He was showing His solidarity with fallen humanity. All through His earthly ministry He showed Himself a friend of tax collectors and sinners, and even at His death 'he was numbered with the transgressors' (Luke 22.37). Here, at the outset, He also took His stand by the side of sinners. It was the beginning of the work that was to be completed at Calvary when He was made sin on our behalf (2 Cor. 5.21).

At His baptism Jesus heard a voice and saw a vision. The voice was the call for which He had been waiting—the call to commence His ministry, while the vision was of a dove—the symbol of the Holy Spirit descending upon Him and endowing Him for Messiahship.

In New Testament times it was customary for Jewish proselytes to be baptized when they forsook heathendom and allied themselves with the people of God. There was something quite distinctive, however, about John's baptism. It was no mere ceremonial purification, but signified 'repentance for the remission of sins'. Furthermore, it was for Jews and not merely proselytes, and, most important of all, it was closely linked with preparation to meet the coming Messiah.

It is significant that, according to John's teaching, neither the observance of religious rites, nor a godly ancestry, are of any avail in providing for the sinner a way of escape from the divine judgement. None can opt out of the need of repentance. The two operative words for the seeking sinner are 'repent' and 'believe'.

75: Behold the Lamb!

John 1.19–34

The main theme of this passage is the witness of John the Baptist to Christ. The priests and Levites who came to John represented the religious life of the community. John was emphatic in pointing out he was not the Christ. Even the baptism that he gave was not comparable with His baptism. John's ministry consisted in preaching repentance and in pointing to the Christ, who was so much greater than he.

It is clear that the Jewish leaders regarded John as a very important person. He might have been the Messiah himself, or the prophet Elijah who was expected to appear, or 'the Prophet' whom some equated with Jeremiah. John was emphatic with his disclaimers—he was himself, and his mission was to bear witness to the Messiah. At the same time, he did not decry the importance of his own ministry. He was the Messiah's herald, and as such should be heeded. He was, in fact, the last of the Old Testament prophets, and in the assessment of Christ Himself, 'the greatest born of woman'. Whereas we must not over-rate ourselves, there is no value in self-depreciation. Each of us has a place to fill and John recognized his. He was concerned to point men to Jesus, whom he described as 'the Lamb of God'. This phrase conveys the thought of sacrifice, and John in using it anticipates Christ's atoning death on the Cross.

It seems from this passage that John had already baptized Jesus, and he had been led by prophetic insight to recognize Him as the Messiah—the One who would baptize with the Holy Spirit in due time. When John saw Jesus approaching him He recognized Him immediately. Though cousins they had probably not met until recently. John had spent his life in the seclusion of the desert, whereas Jesus had been in Galilee. It could well be that the two had not met until Jesus came to Jordan to be baptized by John. John expected that there would be some indication whereby he would recognize the Messiah, and as Jesus emerged from the Jordan the long-expected sign was given—the Spirit descended on Him from heaven like a dove. John the Baptist stands for all time as a shining example of what every Christian's witness should be. He was ready to stand aside and point to Christ rather than seek glory for himself.

76: The Forerunner

John 3.1–8; 3.22–4.3

Nicodemus was a scrupulous observer of the law, a Pharisee held in the highest esteem, and a ruler of the Jews. Nevertheless, he was fairly open-minded in certain respects. He had been intrigued by what he had heard about the teaching and miracles of Jesus of Nazareth and was eager to investigate for himself. He was even willing to admit that only a truly godly man could act in this way.

Our Lord met Nicodemus with a challenge—in spite of his

religious upbringing and position of leadership, he needed to be born anew. He could see beneath the surface and could discern Nicodemus' deep spiritual need, for all his outward religious profession. In effect Jesus was saying: 'God's mysteries are not the heritage of the learned, the moral, or the religious, simply because of learning, morality or religion; they are the heritage of the spiritually transformed' (Tenney).

Nicodemus was obviously nonplussed at this reference to new birth. He could think of birth along physical lines (4), but that could not be what Christ meant. At the same time how could a man at his time of life start all over again? Our Lord's words in reply to Nicodemus' query have been the subject of much discussion, particularly his reference to water. Was our Lord referring here to baptism? There are other New Testament references where water and Spirit are mentioned together in relation to baptism (cf. John 1.33; Matt. 3.11). Christ's teaching makes it clear that water baptism of itself is not sufficient. The sign needs to be accompanied by the thing signified—namely, the cleansing work of the Holy Spirit.

Following the interview Jesus and His disciples resorted to the country district of Judea and baptized, although our Lord did not Himself baptize (4.2). Meanwhile, further north, John was continuing to baptize those who came to him in repentance. Clearly, even at this early stage in His work, Jesus felt that baptism was of great importance. In common with John's baptism it would have been a sign of repentance but would have had the added dimension that here was One who was to baptize not only with water, but with the Spirit (cf. Mark 1.8). Although the full significance of Christian baptism could not emerge until after Christ's death, resurrection and ascension, and the coming of the Spirit at Pentecost, the baptism which Jesus and His disciples practised should be regarded 'as a guarantee of greater blessing to come' (Tasker). Already, however, baptism is taking on the character of an outward sign of an inward change ('being born of water and the Spirit', v. 5) and a public confession of the participant's identification with Christ and His Kingdom.

77: Misdirected Ambition
Mark 10.35–45; Luke 12.49–53

In this passage we have highlighted the unfortunate ambition of two of our Lord's disciples, James and John. Although they had lived so close to Him they had obviously failed to take heed both of His teaching and example. While He is about to lay down His very life, they are concerned with self-interest—seeking to ensure a place of prominence in the coming Kingdom. Jesus has to tell them sadly that they do not realize what they are asking. They have failed to realize that leadership in His Kingdom only comes to those who are prepared to suffer.

The word 'baptism' is used here by our Lord in a metaphorical sense. The cup stands for suffering and the baptism for overwhelming sorrow. Baptism is used in the Old Testament as a picture of one undergoing the wrath of God (Psa. 69.15). Christian baptism is 'into Christ's death' (Rom. 6.3), and is a reminder of the costliness of discipleship. Every disciple must, in some measure, drink from Christ's cup of sorrow and share in His baptism of suffering, and this very fact cuts right across the spirit which James and John were displaying in their attempt to secure personal glory.

Our Lord never left His followers in any doubt as to what it might mean to serve Him. He had not come to bring peace but a sword, and even within the confines of a family there might be friction and strife. Once more He uses the metaphor of baptism. He has 'an overwhelming baptism to come' (Berkeley). Baptism here must refer to the coming passion (cf. Mark 10.38f.). It has been said that the thought of Calvary was already a Gethsemane to the Lord. It is impossible to exaggerate the suspense and agony of anticipation (12.50).

Those of us who live in countries where we are spared from physical persecution for the sake of Christ need to remember our brothers who suffer for His sake. Even so, some of us may know in our own experience how becoming a Christian has caused a division in the family. We should not be surprised at this for we have been repeatedly warned that Christ came not 'to give peace on earth, but rather division'. Countless numbers of Christians across the world have experienced what it is to be baptized with this baptism.

78: Baptism in the Early Church

Acts 2.37–42; 8.9–13, 35–38

Peter's preaching on the Day of Pentecost brought about deep conviction in the hearts of his hearers. To those who truly repented Peter addressed a call to be baptized as a sign of their

105

repentance and as a confession of their new-found faith in Jesus as Messiah. With this double demand for repentance and baptism he held out a double offer—the remission of their sins and the gift of the Holy Spirit. Baptism was to be in the name of Jesus—a clear indication that it signified an identification with Him, in His suffering and resurrection, in His present life and in the ethical and practical demands of His gospel. Four characteristics marked the life of these new converts—they showed a deep and continuing interest in the apostles' teaching; they entered into fellowship with one another; they obeyed Christ's injunction to remember Him in breaking of bread, and attended public prayer (42).

In the second passage we are introduced to the situation before Philip began his work in Samaria. Simon Magus was a magician who indulged in a good deal of self-advertisement and also in sorcery. He had remarkable success but his aims and motives were for his own glory rather than the glory of God. When Philip arrived on the scene, Simon believed and was baptized. We are bound to ask whether his motives were mixed, for he shows a certain amount of self-interest and later has an unhealthy concern for the more spectacular demonstrations of the Spirit's presence and the power which they would bring him. His belief that he could purchase the Spirit demonstrates a lack of understanding.

It was clearly possible in the Early Church for people to be baptized from wrong motives or without an adequate appreciation of the significance of the action. Baptism should never be undertaken lightly by those who make a profession of faith. It is a solemn, and in some senses irrevocable, step; a public and personal declaration of our faith in Christ, love for Him and determination to follow Him whatever the cost, a symbolic act which should be a means of cementing our relationship with Him and drawing strength from Him.

In the story of the baptism of the Ethiopian eunuch we have an example of the stages which would normally precede baptism. The eunuch was an honest seeker after truth—he was searching the Scriptures and through the illumination of the Holy Spirit he was brought face to face with Jesus Christ. It is clear that he must have repented of his sin there and then and turned to Christ as Saviour. With the minimum of delay he sought baptism. At the time of his baptism the eunuch could have known little theology, but he had a clear grasp of his own condition and of what Christ had done for him. He had believed and that fact was enough to warrant Philip baptizing him. No doubt Philip had told him about baptism as being the way by which new converts may confess their faith in Christ, and express their identity with Him. That being so, the eunuch's desire is natural and Philip's willingness to baptize him shows the importance attached to baptism by the Early Church as a sign of entry into the Kingdom.

79: Converts Baptized

Acts 16.11–15, 25–34

Ramsay comments, 'It is remarkable with what interest Luke records the incidents from harbour to harbour. He has the true Greek feeling for the sea.' Neapolis was the harbour of Philippi. The Roman colonies were primarily intended as military safeguards and were, in fact, representations in miniature of the Roman people. Philippi contained no synagogue and practically no Jews. It was a military rather than a commercial centre. Those who were Jews or Jewish proselytes were accustomed to gather for prayer by a riverside. Among the company on this occasion was Lydia, a native of Thyatira, which was famous for its dyeing. The fact that she traded in purple-dyed garments suggests that she was a woman of position and means. She was herself a Jewish proselyte, and seems to have had an influence over her whole household. It is interesting to note the different ways in which men and women are converted in Acts. In the case of the Philippian jailer there was an element of fear, in the case of Saul conversion was a most dramatic experience, whereas Lydia simply 'opened her heart'.

In common with the other converts of whom we read in Acts, Lydia lost no time in seeking baptism. Furthermore, members of her household were baptized with her. It has, of course, long been a point of discussion as to whether there were any children involved.

It is remarkable that Paul and Silas were able to sing when they had been so cruelly wronged and were cooped up in a stifling cell in the utmost discomfort. Their wounds had not been treated and they had been left without food. When the earthquake struck, the prisoners were terrified, and seemed to make no attempt to escape. Paul and Silas alone remained self-possessed. The jailer was filled with fear, and on the point of suicide until restrained by Paul. He asks the momentous question, 'What must I do to be saved?'

And the answer he immediately received was simple and authoritative—salvation demands faith in a person, and even faith itself is a free gift of God's grace. As in the case of Lydia, so here the household is included. The reality of the jailer's conversion was expressed in a most practical way for he immediately washed the wounds of his prisoners, and he too was baptized 'with all his family' without delay. Here again, it must remain an open question as to whether all who were baptized with him consciously heard, understood and personally responded to the preaching of the gospel.

80: Baptism in the Name of the Lord Jesus

Acts 19.1–7

Paul, having visited the churches of south Galatia now pays a return visit to Ephesus. He soon came across a number of professing disciples who appeared to be entirely ignorant of the existence of the Holy Spirit. Some have suggested they may not have been Christians at all, but this would seem unlikely in view of the fact that they are called disciples. Furthermore, Paul asked them if they received the Holy Spirit when they believed, indicating that he took them to be true believers. It could be, of course, that the apostle was mistaken. They had, in fact, been disciples of John the Baptist, and it is hard to think that they had no knowledge whatever of the Holy Spirit, but certainly they were not conscious of His active presence. They had been baptized by John the Baptist and it is important to remember that his was a baptism of expectation rather than fulfilment. Now they are baptized into the name of the Lord Jesus, and when Paul laid his hands on them they received the gift of the Holy Spirit with outward manifestations. These twelve disciples perhaps became the nucleus of the Ephesian church.

Receiving the Holy Spirit is a subject which causes a great deal of discussion. It is clear from the Acts that every believer shares in the gift of the Spirit. The confession of Jesus as Lord is the unfailing sign of the Spirit's presence (1 Cor. **12**.3). There are, in fact, four outstanding instances in the Acts of believers 'receiving the Holy Spirit' (**2**.1–4; **8**.14 ff; **10**.44–48; **19**.1–7). In each case a number of believers were involved, and in most cases certain unusual manifestations followed. We suggest that in these instances it was clearly necessary that there should be an

immediate proof that He had, in fact, been received. The time
and manner of the Spirit's coming differed, however, in each case.
In one case the Spirit came before baptism, in two cases after
baptism, and in two cases through the laying on of hands of an
apostle. Paul makes it clear 'Anyone who does not have the
Spirit of Christ does not belong to him' (Rom. 8.9). Every true
believer is indwelt by the Holy Spirit, but we are told to be filled
with the Spirit (Eph. 5.18). Incidentally, this incident in Acts
ch. 19 is the last occasion on which we read of the Holy Spirit
being given and of those receiving Him speaking with tongues.

81: Baptism into Christ

Romans 6

In the early chapters of Romans Paul has been primarily concerned with the subject of justification by faith—how the sinful
are accounted righteous because of Christ's atoning sacrifice
solely on the basis of saving faith. He now turns to the subject
of holy living, dealing with those who might be tempted to argue,
'If God's grace abounds and triumphs so wonderfully, let us go
on sinning so as to bring out that grace more and more.' In
refuting any such notion the apostle points out that pardon is to
be seen as the cause and producer of holiness. In pursuing this
argument Paul introduces the subject of baptism.

He speaks of believers as being baptized into Christ (cf. Gal.
3.27). Baptism is seen as a symbol of our death and burial with
Christ. A. B. Simpson comments: 'There must be an actual
yielding of the life to be crucified with Christ. There is a moment
when we consent to die. . . . It is assumed by the apostle that we
did this in our baptism.' While the rite of baptism pictures our
death and burial it does not bring it about. We may be partakers
of the outward seal and yet lack the inward reality.

But Christ did not remain buried, He rose to a new life; so it
should be with His people. Those who see themselves as having
died with Christ, by faith, identify themselves also with His
resurrection. The same supernatural power which raised Christ
from the dead is available to Christians to enable them to walk
in newness of life (4). A Christian shares the death of Christ—but
more than that, he also shares His resurrection.

Those Christians who feel that the only valid form of baptism is by immersion base their arguments very largely on this passage. They point out that only when the candidate is totally immersed does he really enact what it means to be buried with Christ. If, as many would feel, the passage refers to water baptism, it is clear that the apostle assumed that every professing Christian would have been baptized. Baptism is seen to signify union with Christ. The phrase frequently used in the New Testament is 'baptized into Christ', or 'into the name of Christ' (Acts **8.16**; **19.5**; Gal. **3.27**). Union with Christ, invisibly effected by faith, is visibly signified and sealed by baptism. Just as being immersed represents burial with Christ, so coming up out of the waters of baptism represents the believer entering into newness of life. Thus a Christian, by faith inwardly and by baptism outwardly, has been united to Christ in His death and resurrection.

82: The Symbolism of Baptism

Colossians 2.8–15

In this passage the apostle is expressing his anxiety for the churches at Colossae and Laodicea and calling upon them to be steadfast in the face of false teaching. There were those who taught that no Gentile could become a Christian without first becoming a Jew and submitting to circumcision, the outward sign of covenant relationship with God. Paul argues that all that has now changed. God has established a new covenant, the symbol of which is baptism. Circumcision marked the entry into the covenant people of God for the Jew and remained a perpetual reminder of his status as one set apart for, and dedicated to, God —baptism fulfils this role for the Christian, illustrating the spiritual change which has taken place. Verses 12, 13 are reminiscent of Rom. 6.4–6 which might be regarded as a commentary on this passage.

Paul is concerned once again to underline the change involved in conversion and baptism. Once dead, we are now alive (13) with a life which has all the richness and fullness of God's life (9, 10). Baptism should not be seen only as a once-for-all act— it is a symbol of the new life we share with God from day to day. Paul warns the Colossians against putting a trust in any physical action if the inward reality of a new life is missing—each day must be a conscious expression of this inward life.

In vs. 14, 15 Paul points out that all legal observances were abolished in Christ. Christ, by His death, cancelled the bondage which sinful men otherwise would have to face. Jew and Gentile alike had the law of conscience in their hearts and both were equally guilty. The Mosaic Law had its decrees and ordinances and the duty of the Jew was even heavier. Nevertheless, at the Cross the account had been settled once and for all. Satisfaction has been made—our sentence of death has been nailed to Christ's Cross. The bond has been nailed to the Cross, just as a cancelled bond is often stuck on a file—it is marked 'paid'—'wiped out'.

To sum up Paul's teaching—a believer, through his faith, is identified with Christ, and by the Holy Spirit he is baptized into union with Christ. The symbol of this union is baptism in water, which witnesses to his union with Christ in death and resurrection. The forgiveness which the Christian enjoys is not offered without full payment of the debt. As the result of union with Christ we are completely delivered from any subjection to 'principalities and powers' (15). By the cross He 'publicly exposed them to disgrace' (Berkeley).

Christ is the one all-sufficient Saviour, because of who He is (9, 10), and because of what He has done (13–15). Any teaching in whatever language it is presented which detracts from the person and work of Christ is palpably false (8).

Questions and themes for study and discussion on Studies 74–82.

1. What was the special significance of John's baptism (Luke 3)?
2. What was the relationship between conversion and baptism in the early Church?
3. What were the particular differences between John's baptism and Christian baptism as seen in Acts 19.1–7?
4. In what sense may we regard baptism as a visual aid (Rom. 6)?
5. Do you see any connection between circumcision under the Old Covenant and baptism under the New?

111

CHARACTER STUDIES

83: Grace Abounding

1 Timothy 1

This is obviously the chapter from which John Bunyan took the title for his autobiography: *Grace Abounding to the Chief of Sinners.* The chapter is itself notably autobiographical. If nothing else of the New Testament had survived it would be possible from this score of verses to guess that an outstanding man had been redeemed from a career of violence and hatred against God, who, in Christ Jesus, had offered salvation to the world. In that Name, Paul under divine commission, had proclaimed the gospel, and had founded churches in two continents. And already the purity of the message was challenged by those who promulgated false doctrine, dishonouring to God, and complicating a primitive simplicity.

This is the first of the three Pastoral Epistles, a title in use for the last two centuries, and in the name there is indication of the problems of the expanding Church and the new considerations which were occupying Paul's mind. Timothy appears to be in charge at Ephesus, and Paul seems to write from Macedonia. It is a fair guess that he had been released from his first imprisonment in Rome, and had four or five years' activity of which nothing is recorded. Perhaps he went to Spain during this interval. He was certainly busy, and busy with a new urgency.

He could see, at any rate after the summer of 64, that grim days were coming, not only for Rome, increasingly restive under Nero, but also for the Church. It was no time for nonsense, with heretical teachers making difficulties for the Christian community with strange perversions, fables, genealogies, and those manifold perversions of God's truth in which the imagination of deviant theologies and pseudo-intellectualism, no less than the exponents of exotic cults of 'experience', have always been fertile.

Moreover, Paul could see that organization was a prime necessity. The old coherence of love and mutual fellowship in the Christian groups obviously needed the reinforcement of discipline. Leadership of a tried and tested sort had to be established, and Paul's letters to Timothy and Titus are full of his rapid and concise directions. Crisis was in his mind, and critics, assault and sabotage, could only be met by a proper ordering of defence. It is the same Paul, and yet a new Paul who confronts us, a man convinced that time is short, and that nothing in the world, his own life included, mattered so much as the continued functioning and endurance of the Church he had given toilsome and perilous years to found.

*84: The Elder

1 Timothy 3.1–7; Titus 1

We first see in these chapters the picture of men who are to march through the centuries—the leaders of the church. There are saints among them, the salt of the earth. There are martyrs and heroes —and there are John Masefield's 'princes and prelates with periwigged charioteers, riding triumphantly laurelled to lap the fat of the years . . .' But whatever the worth or the worthlessness of men have made of honourable office, the portrait is clear, and among the ideal characters of Scripture must stand the elder, the deacon and the minister.

It seems likely that, in the New Testament, the bishop (or overseer) and the elder are identical. Paul was eager to see, above all, good, sane, upright men in control. The senior officer must be a man of blameless reputation, a 'man of one woman', as v. 2 puts it. He must be alert, self-controlled, with open home, a good teacher. He must not mar his testimony either by drunkenness, or violence, or money-grabbing—a man, in short, of dignity and obvious integrity. No bad-tempered bully, greedy, unable to exercise a proper discipline among his own, can qualify.

The verses in the parallel passage in the letter to Titus which correspond to vs. 6 and 7 omit the corresponding directions. Paul's magnificent common sense saw that what applied to an old urban community, where the church was well-established, might not equally apply in the primitive island community of Crete. The responsible officer must not be 'a new shoot', he says. The word is used in the Septuagint, the Greek Old Testament, for newly planted trees (Psa. 144.12). A man too immature and thrust into office, might be more easily tempted to damaging pride in a place like Ephesus, than among the simpler people of Crete.

Note that Paul expects his elder to hold a good testimony with the world outside the church. Abraham reminded Lot that 'the

113

Canaanite and the Perizzite dwelt in the land' (Gen. **13**.7f). The non-Christian pays the Church the unwitting compliment of knowing what the Christian ought to be, and expecting it. Add these qualities together, picture the character which emerges, and you have the fair ideal. It would be hard to say that it has never been completely attained. Ideals would cease to be ideals, were they too easily in reach. Such, at any rate, is the elder—the bishop, or what you will.

*85: The Deacon

1 Timothy 3.8–16

The deacons were the lesser serving officers of the church. They must be worthy of respect, dignified. The AV(KJV) 'grave' seems to contain some of the Roman virtue of 'gravity', the Stoic 'reserve', which Paul may have admired. In a modern setting the word suggests a thoughtful avoidance of extremes in demeanour, dress and speech, a freedom from frivolity and extravagance, above all from exhibitionism, the common temptation of all office holders in any sphere of authority.

Above all the good deacon is not double-tongued. He avoids the reprehensible adaptation of one mode of address for one person, another for another. He is plainly truthful, never deceitful and insincere in what he says. This does not mean he is a man of brutal and hurtful frankness, nor devoid of the common courtesies and graceful proprieties of conversation. It merely forbids a form of falsehood and hypocrisy. The deacon also must be no addict of the bottle or the money-bag.

Then comes (9) simplicity and sincerity in belief, allied to like qualities in speech. A clear conscience forbids reservations in belief. The unsure, the uncommitted and the unconvinced are not men for office. The church can only be safely led by men who believe every word they say. The tragedy of recent years has been the easy victory won by a small band of liberal theologians over churchmen of feeble faith—the group whom someone has dubbed 'the Munich school of theologians', ready to sell the pass in the weak belief that they can hold some vague position, if only their own, somewhere in the lower foothills, and too busy listening to their enemies to say anything useful to their friends. No one should function in the Church, in any mode of leadership, save men of muscular faith, and sturdy conviction. Such men must be

114

chosen only after long scrutiny (10). And such men depend upon good wives. All men do, for good or ill . . .

It is another fine picture of men who should be common in the Christian Church. Those who thus qualify and serve, 'have won for themselves high standing, and the right to speak openly on the Christian faith' (13). No others have.

86: The Young Minister

1 Timothy 4

The good minister, as Paul envisages him, with Timothy and Ephesus in mind, must function in the midst of a hostile world and a church infiltrated by the enemy. He must, above all, know where he stands and speak with conviction. 'In setting these matters before the church, you will be a good minister (servant) of Jesus Christ, ever nourishing yourself on the words of the faith and the good doctrine you have followed.' Weakness in a ministry, weakness in a church, comes from weakness in the exposition and study of the Word. And such weakness stems from a decayed faith, and a diminished concept of biblical authority. 'Minister', it must be remembered, is the Latin for slave or servant. It is the opposite of 'magister' or master, the antonym which has survived only in derivatives in English. To lead, we must serve. It is a fundamental law.

'Turn away from the babbling of old women,' Paul tells Timothy with a touch of impatience, 'and exercise yourself rather for godliness.' If we had Timothy's letter to Paul we might understand this remark a little better. Perhaps some dissident women's group was making the young man's task difficult. 'Bodily exercise,' he goes on, 'has its minor place of usefulness, but godliness is of all-round value, containing as it does the promise of life here and hereafter (8), and I do want you to believe this (9). This is the whole theme of our toil and endurance . . . So pass it on' (10, 11).

Timothy's ministry emerges from the urgent and insistent advice to be strong and not to be abashed by arrogant women, or arrogant older men. Authority can belong to a young minister, provided he sets, on all occasions, secular and sacred, a good example in speech, in manner of life and in the basic qualities of character set forth in the three nouns which conclude v. 12—love, that is compassion, mercy, tolerance and Christlikeness,

115

faith, that is the sturdiness and steadfastness of Christian conviction, and thirdly, purity, that is personal integrity and self-control. And observe the test of self-discipline which follows. The young minister must be diligent in reading, preaching, study. Timothy was probably in his early thirties. This was Paul's portrait as Paul hoped to see him. and as he no doubt endeavoured to be.

87: The Talkers

1 Timothy 6

There is in this chapter a group to be found at many times and at many places, not only in the church but in all the institutions of democracy—the lovers of talk for the sake of talking, the habitual controversialists, the specialists in discussion for no constructive end, the promoters of vain questionings.

It is interesting to read the various renderings of Paul's strong words about this group at Ephesus. There was many a 'pompous ignoramus' (NEB) in the church, people filled with 'a morbid appetite for discussions and arguments' (Williams), 'quibbling over the meaning of Christ's words and stirring up arguments' (Taylor), from which naturally and inevitably arose, and still arise, 'defamations, quarrellings, wrangling, ill-natured suspicions, recriminations, malicious innuendoes, abusive language, perpetual contention, constant friction, minds warped ...' This grim list is collected from five translations of vs. 4 and 5, checked against the original. Any modern Timothy, plagued in like fashion by the wrong kind of 'discussion groups', can be assured that Paul meant no less.

Paul was no stranger to constructive and necessary controversy. He had fought a good fight against those who corrupted the simplicity of his message. He had 'withstood Peter to his face.' What he deprecated was the old vice of Greek communities with which some who share the democratic and dialectical heritage of the Greeks are not unfamiliar—the habit of exhibitionist talking. The Athenians, said Luke, in an ironical phrase, 'spent their time in nothing else but either to tell or to hear some new thing' (Acts 17.21). In vs. 3 and 4 note the metaphor of health and sickness. These folk were sick, 'morbidly preoccupied', or as the RSV puts it 'with a morbid craving for controversy and for disputes about words'.

The fact that Paul next reverts to riches and their snare, may suggest that the questioners of sound doctrine were the affluent of the congregation, which produced the sect of the Nicolaitans, a group we shall soon be meeting. Some find it convenient to justify a self-willed position by the cover of a privately interpreted text.

88: Two Men
2 Timothy 1.1–15

We have met Timothy before, observed his rural origin, and the formative influence in his life of a Christian mother and grandmother. It is strange to see that the Church was already housing a third generation of Christians. In this chapter, with no sense of incongruity or division, age meets youth. Paul may have been in his sixties. Timothy was probably half that age. Paul, supremely trusting, had left the somewhat nervous, dependent and not very robust young man in charge of the Christian congregation in the great Asian centre of commercialized religion, and religious vice.

He is handing on the torch, and in his words of encouragement to his young successor Paul shows the manner of men both were. Note the open-hearted affection. To be aloof, critical, gruff or impatient with youth, is not of Christ. Youth is the inevitable successor. It is inevitable that the passing of the years will make it certain that other hands will hold the helm, and other minds will plan. If the tradition is to abide intact and fruitfully developing, those other hands, those other minds must be trained and accept the training. To embitter and frustrate is not service to the cause, which must continue. The 'generation gap' can be dug from both sides. Paul was aware of no separation.

Gently, and with his habitual tact, he suggests that, for the task of leadership, Timothy required a strength of character which he had determinedly to lay hold of and develop, love which was not soft indulgence, but compassion uncompromising with sin, and a self-discipline which, in strong and balanced sanity, steadied self and others. In the exhortation there appears a picture of what Paul was, and what he thought Timothy capable of becoming. Verse 12 sums up, in one of the finest testimonies of Scripture. Faith grows into knowledge. Steadfastness in belief produces the evidence of personal experience. Doubt can certainly attack any Christian, but doubt cannot be a way of life, and is a malady which should seek healing.

117

Paul had a load on his heart. Some in the province where he had worked so well, had turned on their old leader. There were tongues of disloyalty wagging, like those of Phygelus and Hermogenes, mere names, but set in a context of shame. Paul trusts Timothy to stand. To break a chain of witness which, with every Christian, goes back to Christ in truest 'apostolic succession', is a sin most grievous.

89: Onesiphorus
2 Timothy 1.16–18; Matthew 25.34–40

The tiny cameo pictures of Bible characters are supremely interesting. Some, as we have seen, in the province of Asia, had turned from Paul. Not so the patron of all prison visitors, Onesiphorus. As Christ had done, long years before, the good man of Ephesus had 'sought Paul out and found him'. Paul's second imprisonment was no honourable house-arrest. It was not without its danger to be associated with him. In the teeming metropolis of a million souls by the Tiber, Onesiphorus sought diligently until he located the prison, and brought Paul refreshment of soul.

There is worth and beauty in such friendship, and honour in standing by a friend in distress. In his moving confession, *De Profundis*, Oscar Wilde tells a story of a friend. Oscar Wilde was no Paul. He fell grievously and suffered deeply, but a moment's act of courtesy brought him near to God. He tells the story thus: 'When I was brought down from my prison to the Court of Bankruptcy, between two policemen,——(Wilde omits the name) waited in the long dreary corridor that, before the whole crowd, whom an action so sweet and simple hushed into silence, he might gravely raise his hat to me, as, handcuffed and with bowed head, I passed him by. Men have gone to heaven for smaller things than that. It was in this spirit, and with this mode of love, that the saints knelt down to wash the feet of the poor, or stooped to kiss the leper on the cheek. I have never said one single word to him about what he did. I do not know to the present moment whether he is aware that I was even conscious of his action. It is not a thing for which one can render formal thanks in formal words. I store it in the treasure-house of my heart. I keep it there as a secret debt that I am glad to think I can never possibly repay. It is embalmed and kept sweet by the myrrh and cassia of many tears.'

Onesiphorous did more for Paul. What happened to him? Did Rome's climate claim his life, as it nearly did that of Epaphroditus? It is thought that he died. Did his visit cost him liberty and life? Paul prays for his family and trusts that Onesiphorus found mercy with the Lord. The phrase is hard to understand for Paul could have had no doubt of the acceptance of such a saint. It remains a mystery, but here was a man who was kind in Ephesus and kind in Rome, who was a blessing when all was secure, and no different when the air was rank with death and danger. Such souls are rare.

90: Self-portrait

2 Timothy 2.1–13; 3.10–17

Paul inevitably wrote of himself in the three word pictures of the second chapter. Rome was full of soldiers in A.D. 67. Anyone who could read the signs could see that the Empire was moving fast towards the civil strife of 69. The city garrison had set up the last two emperors, and were determined not to be outdone by the frontier legions—which, in the end, they were. But as Paul watched Rome's best troops, he saw that to be a soldier a man did what he had done. He had handed over his whole life, was prepared to battle against any odds, to endure discipline, and to be conspicuous.

It was also, he reflected, like being an athlete. At Corinth he could have witnessed the Isthmian Games, the athletes' intensity of effort, the dedication to one end, the striving before a watching crowd. And on many a weary tramp for the gospel's sake, he had seen the peasants of the eastern provinces at work, facing the storms of winter, the mud and the murk, to sow the seed, rejoicing in the harvest, trusting the unseen powers of Nature to bring to growth and to maturity that which they strove so faithfully to plant in the cold, reluctant ground.

He saw that, common to soldier, to athlete, and to farmer, was an end, envisaged and anticipated before the reality, a harvest, a victory. He saw that it all began with a choice involving toil or strife, a continuing in spite of resistance, be it the unyielding soil or the power of the foe. It involved faith in the ultimate, and the overpowering conviction that it is the ultimate in life which counts. He saw that, while farmers and athletes faced their tasks, their tests, their toils alone, the soldier was part of a cohort, a legion, and was held by a common cause and loyalty to his fellows. There was self-discipline, training, defiance of difficulty, sustaining hope, in all three cases.

Paul made no secret of the fact that being a Christian is no easy task. He reminds Timothy that, when as a boy, he threw in his lot with him, he had seen with his own eyes what suffering and persecution had befallen in Timothy's own district—round Iconium and Lystra. There is no easy path in life to any harvest, any victory. Paul knew it. So do we—or if not, as Christians, we soon will learn. But if our society endures, it will be the Christians' doing—and 'never will so much have been owed by so many to so few'.

91: The Last Men
2 Timothy 3.1–9; 4.1–5; 2 Peter 3.1–4

The grim forecast in the opening verses of 2 Tim. 3 looks too familiar for comfort to anyone who watches or reads the news of any day. 'I bring nought for your comfort,' says Paul, as Alfred says, in Chesterton's poem, 'save that the sky grows darker yet, and the sea rises higher.' Here is the picture of a decadent society, the characters of a corrupt age rising like a dank smoke from the prophetic page of Scripture. Watch them march, like the mob in Vanity Fair, across imagination's stage, or if you will, down the city street, the victims of moral breakdown, of the 'permissive society', of triumphant wickedness. Read the passage in several versions: 'they will be proud and contemptuous, without any regard for what their parents taught them': 'they will go to church, yes, but they won't believe a word they hear'; 'they will collect teachers who will tell them what they want to hear'; 'constant liars, thinking nothing of immorality'; 'rough and cruel, sneering at those who try to be good' . . .

Such is the picture Paul sets before his young successor. There have always been such creatures in the world, but it would be blindness indeed not to see their multitude increasing. It is time, if ever time was, to stand firm. And, says Paul, 'you have your Bible'—it 'resets the direction of life'; 'it straightens us out'. 'All Scripture is inspired by God . . .' That, be it noted, is the correct translation. No one with any feeling for Greek, no one, at any rate, who can read Greek without translating it and spelling out its meaning—not a common achievement of commentators—would

120

think the words could be taken in any other way than the RSV and AV(KJV) take them: 'All Scripture is inspired by God and it is profitable for teaching...' And furthermore, anyone with any feeling for the teaching of Paul could not imagine that he would say anything else. The alternative: 'Any scripture which is inspired of God ...' leaves the door open to as many private classifications of Scripture as there are expositors with individual heresies, obsessions, private notions, or what you will. One could imagine Paul's comment.

92: Demas

2 Timothy 4.1–10

Demas is mentioned twice in other contexts—in Col. 4.14, where his name occurs without comment, and in Philem. 24 where he shares the title of fellow-worker. Since both letters went to the same locality, at about the same time, some significance attaches to this. Some years have slipped by, and Demas, seeking what life has to offer, has left his post at Paul's side. 'This world' is the society to which Paul bids us 'be not conformed' in Rom. 12.2, and Demas had found reason to merge with it and make for Thessalonica. There is no evidence that his home was there. Since he is mentioned both to Philemon and the people at Colossae, it might be supposed that he was an Asian, and known in the Lycus valley congregations.

Why did he defect? Life had little left for Paul. To those around him his end seemed certain, and the temptation must have been strong to live and fight another day. Demas did not necessarily abandon the faith, only what Paul thought to be the post of duty. Someone in Thessalonica, parent, friend or one who loved him, may have offered security, even service. There were many who were not in complete agreement with Paul, and with many-edged arguments would press the need for withdrawal.

Or it could have been apostasy. He 'loved the good things of life', says one free translation, and the rendering could be correct. Life has many good things to offer, advantages, pleasures, wealth, popularity, none of which the Christian need deny himself, provided the price is not too high. And the price *is* too high when it involves integrity, testimony, loyalty to God or good, duty or anything else held or professed in the Sacred Name. Paul thought that Demas had paid far beyond his means.

Luke saw fit to stay, and so did Mark, for all the quarrel Paul had once had with him. Both men knew as well as Demas what the situation in Rome held of opportunity, of duty or of peril. They also knew that there was nothing intrinsically evil in physical withdrawal before threat or persecution. It was a case of weighing this against that, and Demas must have added to the scale his measure of disloyalty, self-seeking or regard for self-interest. It is a tiny biography, and it is sad, when history can spare no more than a sentence, to find it thus expressed. If history can grant us this much and no more, what would our sentence be?

Questions and themes for study and discussion on Studies 83–92

1. Does a local church need organization?
2. When is the approval of non-Christians desirable and when is it not?
3. 'The unsure, the uncommitted and the unconvinced are not men for office.'
4. 'Weakness in a ministry, weakness in a church, comes from weakness in the exposition and study of the Word.'
5. The distinction between harmful and necessary controversy.
6. Eliminating the 'generation gap' in the church.
7. Our identification with those in prison for Christ's sake—how can we express it?
8. Is persecution inevitable?
9. The last days—and our days.
10. The troubles of our friends as tests of *our* character.

THE CHURCH'S MINISTRY AND ORDINANCES

The Lord's Supper

Introduction

It is one of the greatest tragedies of the Christian Church that the Lord's Supper, which should be a focal point of the unity of believers, has become the occasion of such disunity. There are Christians who will work and witness with other Christians yet feel unable to join them at the Lord's table.

In the New Testament we find a number of different phrases used to describe this commemorative feast. It is the Lord's Supper (1 Cor. 11.20), the Lord's Table (1 Cor. 10.21), the Breaking of bread (Acts 2.42; 20.7). Some Christians refer to it as a Eucharist (Thanksgiving), while the term Holy Communion derived, no doubt, from 1 Cor. 10.16 is probably the most commonly used expression of all.

93: The Last Supper
Luke 22.1–23

The chapter opens with the account of the treason of Judas. The Day of Unleavened Bread on which the Passover lamb had to be sacrificed, the fourteenth Nisan, saw Peter and John going to prepare for the meal. The householder, no doubt a friend of the Lord's, had a large upper room suitably furnished with cushions spread on the benches. At the appropriate hour just after sunset, Jesus and the disciples reclined on the benches to eat the Passover meal. In the account of this the cup is mentioned first, before the bread. At the Passover four or even five cups were passed round, and all would partake. It is noteworthy that before our Lord passed it to His disciples He paused to give thanks, and in any service of Holy Communion thanksgiving should always play a prominent part. As for our Lord Himself, He makes it clear that He will join in no more festivals till He rejoices in the completed Kingdom. The bread which He took would have been a flat cake of unleavened bread. Verse 20 does

123

not appear in all of the ancient manuscripts, but in the inauguration of the Lord's Supper the bread and the cup are always associated together.

Our Lord introduced the notion of a new covenant or agreement between God and man, of which His blood is the sign and seal. This word covenant calls attention to the federal aspect of the Lord's Supper. Covenants in the Old Testament were associated with covenant signs or seals, and so it is here. They witness to God's promise and pledge, and also to our attitude of acceptance.

When Christ said 'This is my body', He conveyed the idea that in the bread was an emblem of His body, and, similarly, the cup represents the new covenant which is to be sealed and ratified with His blood. Our Lord was speaking to Jews and it would have been unthinkable for them to drink literal blood (Lev. 3.17; 7.26).

It does seem as though Judas Iscariot was one of those who received the Lord's Supper, yet he was a 'son of perdition'. We all need to heed the warning to examine ourselves before we take part in such a service (1 Cor. 11.28–30).

94: A Word of Warning

1 Corinthians 10.14–22

Some Corinthian Christians had been accepting invitations to dine in the homes of their pagan neighbours. Not infrequently they would be presented with food which previously had been offered in sacrifice in a heathen temple. Paul has no objection to their accepting this hospitality, although he does warn that they should be careful to consider all the issues involved (27–30). When, however, it was a question of taking part in a meal explicitly linked with pagan worship (perhaps demanded by their membership of a trade-guild or other official body) it was a different matter. Heathen worshippers would feel that in eating meat or drinking wine which had formed part of a sacrifice they were in some sense identifying themselves with the deity. It was much the same in ancient Israel. In the Jewish ritual, the worshippers who ate the remainder of a sacrifice became 'partners in the altar' (18). The underlying idea here is that to feast on food offered in sacrifice is to have a ceremonial link with the deity at whose altar the food has been presented. Paul is calling upon

Christians to dissociate themselves completely from idol feasts. There can be no compromise in this respect.

The 'bread' and the 'cup' are regarded as things parallel to the food and wine of a pagan sacrifice meal. As was the sacred meal to the Israelite or the idol feast to the heathen worshipper in contemporary Corinth, so is the Supper of the Lord to the Christian.

The 'cup of blessing' was the name given to the third cup in the Passover feast and it may be assumed that this was the cup used by our Lord in instituting the Last Supper. A prayer of thanksgiving would be offered over the cup. A single loaf of bread would have been used and this in itself symbolized the unity of believers in Christ.

The main point the apostle is bringing out here is that feeding at the table of the Lord means having fellowship with Him as well as with His people, whereas participation in an idol feast means having fellowship with demons, and the two are incompatible. It is not enough to regard idols as being of no significance— heathen worship is offered to superhuman powers and seeks to establish communion with them and must, therefore, be taken seriously. God is a jealous God and seeks the entire devotion of His people.

95: The Need for Self-examination

1 Corinthians 11.17–34

This is probably the earliest account we have of the institution of the Lord's Supper. The apostle is concerned to correct certain abuses which had crept into the local observance of the Supper. Instead of being a blessing to the church, the service was having a disruptive effect. A party spirit had crept in and the essential purpose of the Lord's Supper was being overlooked. Differences between rich and poor were being accentuated. The common meal was a travesty of an *agape*, a love-feast. Each ate the food he had brought with him and the rich and the poor did not share their meal. Some were even drunk.

We cannot be sure just what the apostle means when he says he received from the Lord the command relating to the institution of the Lord's Supper. It could mean he had a special revelation, but may refer to the fact that he was passing on teaching that emanated from the Lord, having been transmitted through others

125

to him. Paul stresses the poignancy of the fact that the institution of the Supper took place on the very night when the Lord was being betrayed. A number of other interesting points emerge from this passage—the Supper is a means of actual proclamation of the Lord's death; there is grave danger in participating in the Supper without due consideration for its sacred and solemn meaning; there is a close connection between the Supper and the Second Advent.

The point that the apostle emphasizes is that coming to the Lord's Table calls for self-examination (28–29). The word here is also used in connection with the testing of metals. We should not lightly take part in a service of holy communion. Paul is not saying that to participate unworthily will incur eternal damnation, but he is saying that to do so is to bring upon oneself very real punishment, as the Corinthians themselves had done (30). 'Not to discern the body' means to fail to pay due regard to the solemnity of the occasion.

Verses 30–32 have occasioned a great deal of comment. Paul appears to be saying that the reason why some Christians have died and others suffer ill-health is due to a wrong attitude towards this service. Such divine judgement is of the Lord's goodness since otherwise those concerned might find themselves bracketed with the heathen world and sharing in its condemnation. However difficult these verses may be for us to understand, the overall demand for a serious approach comes to us as clearly as to the Corinthians. The two things that matter more than anything else as we come to the Table are that we should be in a right relationship with the Lord and with our fellow believers.

96: Spiritual Eating and Drinking

John 6

The feeding of the five thousand is the only miracle recorded by all four evangelists. John definitely 'dates' the occasion by pointing out that it took place at Passover time (4). He is the only one to record the conversation between the Lord and Philip. Of the four accounts John's is the most graphic for, no doubt, he was present. Needless to say, numerous attempts have been made to rationalize or explain away what was clearly a creative act of divine omnipotence. Our concern is with the significance of the miracle and particularly of Christ's words as recorded in vs. 50,

51. The apostle John saw Christ's miracles as 'signs', having a doctrinal significance and we gather from this that Christ as the Bread of life is adequate to meet the need of every living person. Yet bread has to be appropriated and so men must put their trust in Christ if they are to be satisfied. In passing, it is worth noting that whereas the actual supply of bread was miraculously provided the distribution of it was left to the disciples. God does not do for us what we can do for ourselves or for one another. The wine was miraculously supplied at Cana, but the servants had to fill the water pots. Lazarus was raised from the dead, but men had to remove the grave clothes. Peter was miraculously released from prison, but he had to find his own way to John Mark's house. Samuel Chadwick's comment made many years ago is even more apt today: 'The words, "give ye them to eat" may serve as an eternal rebuke to the helplessness of the Church, face to face with a starving world and regarding her own scanty resources with dismay. In the presence of heathenism, of dissolute cities and of semi-pagan peasantries, she is ever looking wistfully to some far-off supply. And her Master is ever bidding her believe that the five loaves and fishes in her hand, if blessed by Him, will satisfy the famine of mankind.'

Considerable discussion has arisen from our Lord's statement that the bread was His flesh which He was about to give for the life of the world, stressing at the same time the absolute necessity of eating His flesh and drinking His blood in order to enjoy eternal life (51–56). Clearly Christ is pointing forward to His death. This passage, therefore, teaches the absolute necessity for men and women to participate in the atoning death of Christ (as expressed here by giving His flesh and blood) in order to possess eternal life. The spiritual act of appropriation by faith is typified by eating and drinking in the material realm.

Christ's discourse at Capernaum was delivered at least a year before the institution of the Lord's Supper, and, therefore, it's primary interpretation cannot be related to it. Furthermore, His words were addressed largely to the crowd, while the Supper was instituted for the disciples. Our Lord's words in John and the Lord's Supper itself both point to the Cross. Nevertheless it is true that at the Supper our Lord's words spoken so long before at Capernaum may be truly meaningful. As Archbishop Cranmer taught, John 6 does not teach that there is oral feeding in the Sacrament nor spiritual feeding confined to the Sacrament but, spiritual feeding 'in and out of' the Sacrament. We conclude then that our Lord's words at Capernaum do not directly relate to the Lord's Supper, but point to those eternal facts to which the Supper also points—namely, the death of Christ on the Cross and the necessity for personally appropriating the benefits of His passion.

Questions and themes for study and discussion on studies 93–96

1. Trace the connection between the Jewish Passover and the Christian service of Holy Communion.
2. What is to be understood from the metaphors of eating and drinking regarding our relationship to Christ? (John 6).
3. What abiding lessons are there from Paul's teaching regarding eating meat offered to idols? (1 Cor. 10).
4. What is the chief significance of the Lord's Supper? (1 Cor. 11. 23–26).